CAREER IDEAS
◆ IDEAS ◆
for kids who like
MATH

DIANE LINDSEY REEVES

Illustrations by
NANCY BOND

☑® Checkmark Books™

An imprint of Facts On File, Inc.

CAREER IDEAS FOR KIDS WHO LIKE MATH

Checkmark Books
An imprint of Facts On File, Inc.
11 Penn Plaza
New York NY 10001

Library of Congress Cataloging-in-Publication Data

Reeves, Diane Lindsey, 1959–
    Career ideas for kids who like math / Diane Lindsey Reeves;
illustrations by Nancy Bond.
        p.   cm. — (Career ideas for kids who like)
    Includes bibliographical references and index.
    Summary: Discusses math-related occupations such as actuary,
banker, computer consultant, economist, and stockbroker, and
describes how to prepare for them.
    ISBN 0-8160-4095-8 (hardcover : acid-free paper). —
ISBN 0-8160-4096-6 (pbk : acid-free paper)
    1. Mathematics—Vocational guidance—United States—Juvenile literature.
[1. Mathematics—Vocational guidance.   2. Occupations.   3. Vocational
guidance].   I. Bond, Nancy, ill.   II. Title.   III. Series: Reeves, Diane
Lindsey, 1959–   Career ideas for kids who like.
QA10.5.R44   2000
510'.23—dc21   99-30051

For Garon,
Lindsey and Lacey,
who have enriched my life
in countless ways.

ACKNOWLEDGMENTS

A million thanks to the people who took the time to share
their career stories and provide photos for this book:

Lenore Blum
Henk-Jan Brinkman
Ron Bruder
Jon Carver
Stoney Cox
Maia Tedesco Dyke
Craig Leafgren
Ramona Mullahey
B. LaRae Orullion
Randy Pickering
Garon Reeves
Sharon Robinson
Matthew Rosenberg
Amy Steiner Schafrann
Jennifer Sherman

Also, special thanks to the design team of Smart Graphics,
Nancy Bond, and Cathy Rincon for bringing the
Career Ideas for Kids series to life with their creative talent.

Finally, much appreciation and admiration is due to
my editor, Nicole Bowen, whose vision and attention
to detail increased the quality of this project in
many wonderful ways.

CONTENTS

MAKE A CHOICE!

You're young. Most of your life is still ahead of you. How are you supposed to know what you want to be when you grow up?

You're right: 10, 11, 12, 13 is a bit young to know exactly what and where and how you're going to do whatever it is you're going to do as an adult. But, it's the perfect time to start making some important discoveries about who you are, what you like to do, and what you do best. It's the ideal time to start thinking about what you *want* to do.

Make a choice! If you get a head start now, you may avoid setbacks and mistakes later on.

When it comes to picking a career, you've basically got two choices.

CHOICE A

Wait until you're in college to start figuring out what you want to do. Even then you still may not decide what's up your alley, so you graduate and jump from job to job still searching for something you really like.

Hey, it could work. It might be fun. Lots of (probably most) people do it this way.

The problem is that if you pick Choice A, you may end up settling for second best. You may miss out on a meaningful education, satisfying work, and the rewards of a focused and well-planned career.

You have another choice to consider.

CHOICE B

Start now figuring out your options and thinking about the things that are most important in your life's work: Serving others? Staying true to your values? Making lots of money? Enjoying your work? Your young years are the perfect time to mess around with different career ideas without messing up your life.

Reading this book is a great idea for kids who choose B. It's a first step toward choosing a career that matches your skills, interests, and lifetime goals. It will help you make a plan for tailoring your junior and high school years to fit your career dreams. To borrow a jingle from the U.S. Army—using this book is a way to discover how to "be all that you can be."

Ready for the challenge of Choice B? If so, read the next section to find out how this book can help start you on your way.

HOW TO USE THIS BOOK

This isn't a book about interesting careers that other people have. It's a book about interesting careers that you can have.

Of course, it won't do you a bit of good to just read this book. To get the whole shebang, you're going to have to jump in with both feet, roll up your sleeves, put on your thinking cap—whatever it takes—to help you do these three things:

☀ **Discover** what you do best and enjoy the most. (This is the secret ingredient for finding work that's perfect for you.)

- ☼ **Explore** ways to match your interests and abilities with career ideas.
- ☼ **Experiment** with lots of different ideas until you find the ideal career. (It's like trying on all kinds of hats to see which ones fit!)

Use this book as a road map to some exciting career destinations. Here's what to expect in the chapters that follow.

GET IN GEAR!

First stop: self-discovery. These activities will help you uncover important clues about the special traits and abilities that make you *you*. When you are finished you will have developed a personal Skill Set that will help guide you to career ideas in the next chapter.

TAKE A TRIP!

Next stop: exploration. Cruise down the career idea highway and find out about a variety of career ideas that are especially appropriate for people who like math. Use the Skill Set chart at the beginning of each entry to match your own interests with those required for success on the job.

MAKE A DETOUR THAT COUNTS!

Here's your chance to explore up-and-coming opportunities in technology, science, health care, and other fields in combination with your passion for numbers.

Just when you thought you'd seen it all, here come dozens of math ideas to add to the career mix. Charge up your career search by learning all you can about some of these opportunities.

DON'T STOP NOW!

Third stop: experimentation. The library, the telephone, a computer, and a mentor—four keys to a successful career planning adventure. Use them well, and before long you'll be on the trail of some hot career ideas.

WHAT'S NEXT?

Make a plan! Chart your course (or at least the next stop) with these career planning road maps. Whether you're moving full steam ahead with a great idea or get slowed down at a yellow light of indecision, these road maps will keep you moving forward toward a great future.

Use a pencil—you're bound to make a detour or two along the way. But, hey, you've got to start somewhere.

HOORAY! YOU DID IT!

Some final rules of the road before sending you off to new adventures.

SOME FUTURE DESTINATIONS

This section lists a few career planning tools you'll want to know about.

You've got a lot of ground to cover in this phase of your career planning journey. Start your engines and get ready for an exciting adventure!

Career planning is a lifelong journey. There's usually more than one way to get where you're going, and there are often some interesting detours along the way. But, you have to start somewhere. So, rev up and find out all you can about you—one-of-a-kind, specially designed you. That's the first stop on what can be the most exciting trip of your life!

To get started, complete the two exercises described below.

WATCH FOR SIGNS ALONG THE WAY

Road signs help drivers figure out how to get where they want to go. They provide clues about direction, road conditions, and safety. Your career road signs will provide clues about who you are, what you like, and what you do best. These clues can help you decide where to look for the career ideas that are best for you.

Complete the following statements to make them true for you. There are no right or wrong answers. Jot down the response that describes you best. Your answers will provide important clues about career paths you should explore.

Please Note: If this book does not belong to you, write your responses on a separate sheet of paper.

On my last report card, I got the best grade in _____.

On my last report card, I got the worst grade in _____.

I am happiest when _____.

Something I can do for hours without getting bored is _____.

Something that bores me out of my mind is _____.

My favorite class is _____.

My least favorite class is _____.

The one thing I'd like to accomplish with my life is _____.

My favorite thing to do after school is __.

My least favorite thing to do after school is _____.

Something I'm really good at is _____.

Something that is really tough for me to do is _____.

My favorite adult person is _____ because_____.

When I grow up _____.

The kinds of books I like to read are about _____.

The kinds of videos I like to watch are about _____.

GET SOME DIRECTION

It's easy to get lost when you don't have a good idea of where you want to go. This is especially true when you start thinking about what to do with the rest of your life. Unless you focus on where you want to go, you might get lost or even miss the exit. This second exercise will help you connect your own interests and abilities with a whole world of career opportunities.

Mark the activities that you enjoy doing or would enjoy doing if you had the chance. Be picky. Don't mark ideas that you wish you would do, mark only those that you would really do. For instance, if the idea of skydiving sounds appealing, but you'd never do it because you are terrified of heights, don't mark it.

Please Note: If this book does not belong to you, write your responses on a separate sheet of paper.

- ❏ 1. Rescue a cat stuck in a tree
- ❏ 2. Visit the pet store every time you go to the mall
- ❏ 3. Paint a mural on the cafeteria wall
- ❏ 4. Run for student council
- ❏ 5. Send e-mail to a "pen pal" in another state
- ❏ 6. Survey your classmates to find out what they do after school
- ❏ 7. Try out for the school play
- ❏ 8. Dissect a frog and identify the different organs
- ❏ 9. Play baseball, soccer, football, or _____ (fill in your favorite sport)

❏ 10. Talk on the phone to just about anyone who will talk back
❏ 11. Try foods from all over the world—Thailand, Poland, Japan, etc.
❏ 12. Write poems about things that are happening in your life
❏ 13. Create a really scary haunted house to take your friends through on Halloween
❏ 14. Recycle all your family's trash
❏ 15. Bake a cake and decorate it for your best friend's birthday
❏ 16. Sell enough advertisements for the school yearbook to win a trip to Walt Disney World
❏ 17. Simulate an imaginary flight through space on your computer screen
❏ 18. Build model airplanes, boats, doll houses, or anything from kits
❏ 19. Teach your friends a new dance routine
❏ 20. Watch the stars come out at night and see how many constellations you can find
❏ 21. Watch baseball, soccer, football, or _____ (fill in your favorite sport) on TV
❏ 22. Give a speech in front of the entire school
❏ 23. Plan the class field trip to Washington, D.C.
❏ 24. Read everything in sight, including the back of the cereal box
❏ 25. Figure out "who dunnit" in a mystery story
❏ 26. Take in stray or hurt animals
❏ 27. Make a poster announcing the school football game
❏ 28. Think up a new way to make the lunch line move faster and explain it to the cafeteria staff
❏ 29. Put together a multimedia show for a school assembly using music and lots of pictures and graphics
❏ 30. Invest your allowance in the stock market and keep track of how it does
❏ 31. Go to the ballet or opera every time you get the chance
❏ 32. Do experiments with a chemistry set
❏ 33. Keep score at your sister's Little League game

GET IN GEAR!

❏ 34. Use lots of funny voices when reading stories to children

❏ 35. Ride on airplanes, trains, boats—anything that moves

❏ 36. Interview the new exchange student for an article in the school newspaper

❏ 37. Build your own treehouse

❏ 38. Help clean up a waste site in your neighborhood

❏ 39. Visit an art museum and pick out your favorite painting

❏ 40. Play Monopoly® in an all-night championship challenge

❏ 41. Make a chart on the computer to show how much soda students buy from the school vending machines each week

❏ 42. Keep track of how much your team earns to buy new uniforms

❏ 43. Play an instrument in the school band or orchestra

❏ 44. Put together a 1,000-piece puzzle

❏ 45. Write stories about sports for the school newspaper

❏ 46. Listen to other people talk about their problems

❏ 47. Imagine yourself in exotic places

❏ 48. Hang around bookstores and libraries

❏ 49. Play harmless practical jokes on April Fools' Day

❑ 50. Join the 4-H club at your school
❑ 51. Take photographs at the school talent show
❑ 52. Make money by setting up your own business—paper route, lemonade stand, etc.
❑ 53. Create an imaginary city using a computer
❑ 54. Do 3-D puzzles
❑ 55. Keep track of the top 10 songs of the week
❑ 56. Train your dog to do tricks
❑ 57. Make play-by-play announcements at the school football game
❑ 58. Answer the phones during a telethon to raise money for orphans
❑ 59. Be an exchange student in another country
❑ 60. Write down all your secret thoughts and favorite sayings in a journal
❑ 61. Jump out of an airplane (with a parachute, of course)
❑ 62. Plant and grow a garden in your backyard (or windowsill)
❑ 63. Use a video camera to make your own movies
❑ 64. Get your friends together to help clean up your town after a hurricane
❑ 65. Spend your summer at a computer camp learning lots of new computer programs

❑ 66. Build bridges, skyscrapers, and other struc-
tures out of
LEGO®s

❑ 67. Plan a concert in
the park for lit-
tle kids

❑ 68. Collect differ-
ent kinds of
rocks

❑ 69. Help plan a
sports tourna-
ment

❑ 70. Be DJ for the
school dance

❑ 71. Learn how to fly a
plane or sail a boat

❑ 72. Write funny captions for pictures
in the school yearbook

❑ 73. Scuba dive to search for buried treasure

❑ 74. Recognize and name several different breeds of cats,
dogs, and other animals

❑ 75. Sketch pictures of your friends

❑ 76. Pick out neat stuff to sell at the school store

❑ 77. Answer your classmates' questions about how to use
the computer

❑ 78. Draw a map showing how to get to your house from
school

❑ 79. Make up new words to your favorite songs

❑ 80. Take a hike and name the different kinds of trees,
birds, or flowers

❑ 81. Referee intramural basketball games

❑ 82. Join the school debate team

❑ 83. Make a poster with postcards from all the places you
went on your summer vacation

❑ 84. Write down stories that your grandparents tell you
about when they were young

CALCULATE THE CLUES

Now is your chance to add it all up. Each of the 12 boxes on these pages contains an interest area that is common to both your world and the world of work. Follow these directions to discover your personal Skill Set:

1. Find all of the numbers that you checked on pages 9–13 in the boxes below and X them. Work your way all the way through number 84.
2. Go back and count the Xs marked for each interest area. Write that number in the space that says "total."
3. Find the interest area with the highest total and put a number one in the "Rank" blank of that box. Repeat this process for the next two highest scoring areas. Rank the second highest as number two and the third highest as number three.
4. If you have more than three strong areas, choose the three that are most important and interesting to you.

Remember: If this book does not belong to you, write your responses on a separate sheet of paper.

ADVENTURE
❏ 1
❏ 13
❏ 25
❏ 37
❏ 49
❏ 61
❏ 73
Total: _____
Rank: _____

ANIMALS & NATURE
❏ 2
❏ 14
❏ 26
❏ 38
❏ 50
❏ 62
❏ 74
Total: _____
Rank: _____

ART
❏ 3
❏ 15
❏ 27
❏ 39
❏ 51
❏ 63
❏ 75
Total: _____
Rank: _____

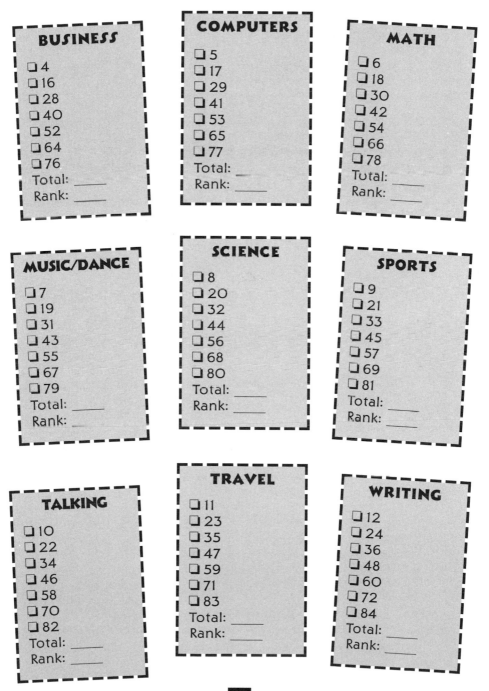

GET IN GEAR!

BUSINESS
- ❏ 4
- ❏ 16
- ❏ 28
- ❏ 40
- ❏ 52
- ❏ 64
- ❏ 76
- Total: _____
- Rank: _____

COMPUTERS
- ❏ 5
- ❏ 17
- ❏ 29
- ❏ 41
- ❏ 53
- ❏ 65
- ❏ 77
- Total: _____
- Rank: _____

MATH
- ❏ 6
- ❏ 18
- ❏ 30
- ❏ 42
- ❏ 54
- ❏ 66
- ❏ 78
- Total: _____
- Rank: _____

MUSIC/DANCE
- ❏ 7
- ❏ 19
- ❏ 31
- ❏ 43
- ❏ 55
- ❏ 67
- ❏ 79
- Total: _____
- Rank: _____

SCIENCE
- ❏ 8
- ❏ 20
- ❏ 32
- ❏ 44
- ❏ 56
- ❏ 68
- ❏ 80
- Total: _____
- Rank: _____

SPORTS
- ❏ 9
- ❏ 21
- ❏ 33
- ❏ 45
- ❏ 57
- ❏ 69
- ❏ 81
- Total: _____
- Rank: _____

TALKING
- ❏ 10
- ❏ 22
- ❏ 34
- ❏ 46
- ❏ 58
- ❏ 70
- ❏ 82
- Total: _____
- Rank: _____

TRAVEL
- ❏ 11
- ❏ 23
- ❏ 35
- ❏ 47
- ❏ 59
- ❏ 71
- ❏ 83
- Total: _____
- Rank: _____

WRITING
- ❏ 12
- ❏ 24
- ❏ 36
- ❏ 48
- ❏ 60
- ❏ 72
- ❏ 84
- Total: _____
- Rank: _____

What are your top three interest areas? List them here (or on a separate piece of paper).

1. _____
2. _____
3. _____

This is your personal Skill Set and provides important clues about the kinds of work you're most likely to enjoy. Remember it and look for career ideas with a skill set that matches yours most closely.

TAKE A TRIP!

Cruise down the
career idea highway and
enjoy in-depth profiles of some of the interesting options in
this field. Keep in mind all that you've discovered about
yourself so far. Find the careers that match your own Skill
Set first. After that, keep on trucking through the other
ideas—exploration is the name of this game.

Math is the cornerstone of some very exciting career
choices. You may already associate with math such careers as
banking and accounting, but others may surprise you. You
can go a long way with a mind filled with mathematical facts
and equations. In fact, math is the main ingredient in a wide
variety of interesting and well-paying careers. Math skills are

in such high demand that 5 of the top-10 careers, according to *Jobs Rated Almanac*, are math related; they are actuary, software engineer, computer analyst, mathematician, and statistician. Math skills also play a significant role in almost every one of the top-50 jobs on the *Almanac*'s list. Together with computers, math is being used in incredible ways in government, business, science, and engineering.

While certainly at the forefront of modern technology and computer advances, mathematics is actually one of the oldest and most basic sciences. It's so old and so important, in fact, that even several centuries ago, important people were singing its praises. Back in the late 1400s, Leonardo da Vinci, one of the world's most famous artists, said that "no human investigation can be called real science if it cannot be demonstrated mathematically." That statement is just as true now as it was then.

Think about it. Without math, how would the ancient Egyptians have created the great pyramids? Without math, how would modern engineers have figured out how to make rockets blast into outer space? Without math, how would researchers develop new lifesaving medicines? Who knows where math will take us next?

As you look through the following career ideas and start investigating others, you will find a lot of overlap among three different areas: math, computers, and science. There are ways to specialize in one without the others, but the most options and opportunities come with a solid base in all three. Future math professionals should take note and stack their school schedule with a strong mix of courses in these three areas.

As you cruise through some of these career ideas, keep in mind that math-related professions offer equal and abundant opportunities for all—regardless of race and gender. Whether you are a girl or a guy, you can succeed in a math career, but first you must do the work. It's as simple as that—for everyone.

Also, as you read about the following careers, imagine yourself doing each job and ask yourself the following questions:

☼ Would I like it?
☼ Would I be good at it?
☼ Is it the stuff my career dreams are made of?

If so, make a quick exit to explore what it involves, try it out, check it out, and get acquainted!

Buckle up and enjoy the trip!

A NOTE ON WEBSITES

Internet sites tend to move around the Web a bit. If you have trouble finding a particular site, use an Internet browser to find a specific website or type of information.

Actuary

WHAT IS AN ACTUARY?

Go ahead, admit it. You don't have a clue about what an actuary actually does, do you? That's OK. Even some adults aren't familiar with this career, although whether they know it or not, most people are affected in some way by the work actuaries do.

The job title actuary makes regular appearances on several "best careers" and "top careers" lists. It routinely makes top 10 and every once in a while shows up in the number-one spot in lists such as *Jobs Rated Almanac's* best jobs in America. This listing ranks jobs according to work environment, salary, availability of jobs, job security, and stress levels. Obviously, the career consistently ranks high in each of these areas in order to retain its winning streak.

According to the Society of Actuaries, actuaries are professionals who are trained in mathematics, statistics, and economic techniques that allow them to put a financial value on future events. It's like putting a price tag on future risks. These risks might include hazards ranging from a natural disaster and its potential impact on a community or industry, to the chances that an average 45-year-old, nonsmoking, overweight male has of suffering a heart attack.

One way to describe what actuaries do is to think of them as financial architects or social mathematicians. They use a unique combination of analytical and business skills to help solve any number of business-related or people-related problems.

In addition to having top-notch math skills, successful actuaries must also be well informed on matters relating to business issues and trends, social science, law, and economics. They must be team players who are comfortable working with all kinds of people, and they must be good communicators—especially when it comes to explaining the complex work they do in simple terms that others can understand. Perhaps, the most important skill is problem solving. Actuaries have to like solving problems and to be good at it too.

At least half of all actuaries practicing in the United States work in the insurance industry where their main function is to figure out how much insurance companies should charge for specific types of insurance policies. Other actuaries work in government helping to manage programs such as Social Security and Medicare. Banks, investment firms, large corporations, accounting firms, and labor unions are other places where actuaries work.

To prepare for a career as an actuary, you will need a college degree. Some actuaries actually major in math or actuarial science, while others major in subjects such as economics, liberal arts, or finance. Whichever route your take, it pays to get a well-rounded education and to pick up good study habits.

In order to achieve professional status, actuaries earn the coveted title of "fellow" in one of the professional societies. To get the best jobs, actuaries must pass a series of tough examinations. Many actuaries start preparing for and taking the initial exams while they are still in college. These exams test basic mathematical skills in areas such as probability, calculus, and algebra, and they are good indications of your aptitude with numbers. Subsequent exams cover topics such as finance, economics, accounting, and insurance law. Experts recommend that actuaries get a few years of experience before tackling these types of exams. Ten years is not an unusual time span for someone to complete all of the exams. Fortunately, once you have landed a job as an actuary, most employers will allow you to use some of your work time to study for the exams, so you get to earn while you learn.

TRY IT OUT

KNOW YOUR NUMBERS
Having a way with numbers is key to the success of an actuary. You can get a head start and have a lot of fun in the process by visiting this interactive website: http://www.cut-the-knot.com. Here you'll find games and puzzles, an inventor's paradox, and lots more. Make sure to give the probability activities a whirl. It will be great practice for your work as an actuary.

For a look at some puzzles that might stump even the most experienced actuary, visit the American Academy of Actuaries' Puzzle Page at http://www.actuary.org/puzzles.htm.

JUST THE FACTS, PLEASE

For the straight scoop on all kinds of math problems, investigate these other websites too.

- ☿ The Math Forum at http://forum.swarthmore.edu
- ☿ Dave's Math Tables at http://www.sisweb.com/math/tables.htm
- ☿ Links to an interesting variety of math sites at http://www.treasure-troves.com/links.html#Math

If all else fails and you still have a question about math, go to the Mathematics WWW Virtual Library at http://euclid.math.fsu.edu/Science/math.html.

EXERCISES FOR THE BRAIN

Two ways to get your brain in the best shape for the rigors of an actuarial career are to work on your math skills and to work on your thinking skills. Here are some software programs published by Knowledge Adventure (located in San Jose, California) that you can use at home. For brain calisthenics try

- ☿ Dr. Brain's Thinking Games: IQ Adventure
- ☿ Dr. Brain's Thinking Games: Puzzles Madness
- ☿ Dr. Brain's Thinking Games: Action/Reaction

To work on your math skills, try

- ☿ Math for the Real World
- ☿ Math Blaster: Algebra
- ☿ Math Blaster: Geometry

You can find these award-winning software programs at most large toy or software stores, or you can shop on-line at http://www.knowledgeadventure.com.

GO FOR THE GOLD

If you want to become an actuary, there is no way around those exams, so you might want to give yourself some practice with the pressure (and pleasure at a job well done) by participating in the USA Mathematical Olympiad Examination. There's one for students in grades 8 or below and one for students in grades 9 and above.

For information write to Dr. Walter E. Mientka at American Mathematics Competitions, University of Nebraska–Lincoln, P.O. Box 81606, Lincoln, Nebraska 68501-1606. Or, if you prefer, call 1-800-527-3690 or visit the American Mathematical Examination website at http://www.unl.edu/amc.

Who knows? You may wind up representing your country at the international competition!

CHECK IT OUT

American Academy of Actuaries
1100 17th Street NW, Seventh Floor
Washington, D.C. 20036
http://www.actuary.org

American Society of Pension Actuaries
4350 North Fairfax Drive, Suite 820
Arlington, Virginia 22203-1619
http://www.aspa.org

Casualty Actuarial Society
1100 North Glebe Road, Suite 600
Arlington, Virginia 22201
http://www.casact.org

International Association of Black Actuaries
1115 Inman Avenue, Suite 235
Edison, New Jersey 08820-1132

Society of Actuaries
475 North Martingale Road, Suite 800
Schaumburg, Illinois 60173
http://www.soa.org

GET ACQUAINTED

Sharon Robinson, Actuary

CAREER PATH

CHILDHOOD ASPIRATION: To be an interior designer or an engineer like her big brother.

FIRST JOB: Cashier at a pharmacy.

CURRENT JOB: Regional actuary for a major property casualty insurance company.

A GOOD GUESS

Sharon Robinson admits that the way she chose her career wasn't exactly scientific. When she was in high school, she read an article called something like "101 Careers You Should Know About." The article listed several math-related careers and gave addresses for more information. Robinson sent letters to some of the organizations mentioned in the article. The only response she got was from the Society of Actuaries, which sent her a packet full of interesting information. She thought the career sounded pretty good, so from that moment on she decided to become an actuary. It's not a method that would work for everyone, but fortunately, it's worked very well for Robinson.

HARDER THAN IT LOOKED

From the very first day of college, Robinson declared her major as actuarial science. The more courses she took, the more she enjoyed it, so she knew she'd made the right choice. She quickly learned that in order to be certified, actuaries have to pass a series of exams. She was doing so well in her courses that she decided to get a head start on the process and sat for the first exam during her first year of college.

Big mistake! It was a disaster. Robinson flunked the exam—badly. Not having had any experience in flunking exams, she was devastated. It took her three tries to pass the first exam, and along the way she learned an important lesson. This was no ordinary exam. By the third round, she had fine-tuned her study process so that she started studying every day—months in advance. She faithfully kept a log of the hours she spent preparing and discovered that 400 hours of study did the trick. That's what it took to pass each exam.

Those exams were the toughest part of the entire process, but Robinson hung in there to pass them and eventually earned the coveted designation of fellow in the Casualty Actuarial Society. The hard work proved worthwhile, because once she completed the exams, she was rewarded with a major job promotion. Even now, her skills and her certification continue to be in high demand.

A GOOD DAY'S WORK

Computers play a big part in Robinson's job as she gathers data on insurance policies for big commercial accounts. Since the accounts she works with can be worth hundreds of thousands of dollars, her decisions have to be based on sound information. For instance, an underwriter may come to her with a client representing a big grocery store chain. Like any other client buying insurance products, this one wants protection so that if something bad happens at one of the stores—if someone gets hurt or gets sued—the grocery store won't go broke trying to fix things.

Robinson's job is to come up with a price that ensures that neither her company or the client loses its shirt if disaster strikes. To do this, Robinson uses the computer to investigate several factors, such as how many claims the grocery story company has made in the past, the overhead expenses of managing the account, and policies provided for similar businesses. Once she gets all the information, she again uses the computer to develop a statistical model that helps her make a decision.

There is a lot at stake if Robinson doesn't do her job accurately, so she works hard to get it right.

A CRYSTAL BALL

Along with determining pricing policies for individual clients and industries, another part of Robinson's job is looking ahead. She reports to the regional president of the company, advising him about trends in the industry and helping determine the company's long-term financial strategy. Some of this work involves taking into consideration worst-case scenarios, such as natural disasters, and analyzing how they would affect the company.

A SATISFYING CAREER

While Robinson enjoys the mathematical challenges of the job, she is quick to point out that it's not just number crunching. The job is very people-oriented and requires her to interface with all kinds, including underwriters, claim handlers, attorneys, and senior managers. She says technical skills alone won't cut it in this work. Good communication skills are key to success as an actuary.

As Robinson has progressed through her career, she's learned what she likes most about the actuary field. Her profession has a very well-defined career track, it is well respected in the insurance industry, and there is an excellent job market.

Sounds like she'd agree with those top career lists!

Automotive Mechanic

WHAT IS AN AUTOMOTIVE MECHANIC?

An automotive mechanic is a highly skilled technician who repairs and services automobiles. People who own cars but don't know how to fix them often consider their automotive mechanic a miracle worker. If you've looked under the hood of a car recently, you'll understand why. Fixing today's sophisticated cars is no job for a rookie.

One of the most important parts of a mechanic's job is diagnosing the problem. A customer might come into a repair shop describing a funny noise that a car is making. The mechanic must take these vague clues and investigate the source of the problem. With newer cars being run by increasingly complex onboard computer systems, the process is likely to involve a combination of high-tech testing and the mechanic's gut instincts about what's gone wrong. In a way, the process is similar to the one that a doctor goes through with a sick patient. In this case, however, the patient is a car.

Some mechanics specialize in servicing a particular type of repair job, such as brakes or transmissions. Others are knowledgeable about (and certified to repair) the major systems of an automobile, including the engine, the transmission, the drive train, the heating and air-conditioning system, the braking system, the electric and electronic systems, and the steering and suspension systems.

Automobiles are a vital part of the modern way of life. People depend on them to get to work, go to school, and run essential errands. However, most people do not have the time or the inclination (not to mention the talent) that it takes to keep a car running in top form on their own. That's why people are willing to pay someone else to do the job.

The best mechanics are those who enjoy working with their hands, have exceptional reasoning skills (here's where some of your math skills come in), and simply love cars. They're the ones who can name every make and model of car going by on a busy road. They're the ones who have a natural knack for taking things apart and putting them back together again. They are also the ones who have completed an auto repair course at a vocational school or other type of educational facility and are willing to keep learning new skills as automotive technology continues to change.

The best jobs go to mechanics who are certified. Certification requires more than 1,000 hours working on cars and passing a written exam. It's a rigorous process, but once completed it says a lot about your skills, your competence, and your commitment to the profession. Being certified helps you earn the trust of employers and customers alike.

As you might have already guessed, mechanics fix more than just cars. Depending on their training and experience, a mechanic might specialize in repairing big trucks, buses, motorcycles, trains, boats, or airplanes. Since these repair technicians tend to be highly skilled in some pretty tricky technical areas, these careers are in big demand and offer the potential for some fairly high earnings.

You can count on finding a good job as a mechanic if you get the training you need and prove yourself as a reliable and skilled technician. This profession often suffers from severe shortages of qualified workers, so as long as there are cars on the road, there will be jobs for qualified mechanics.

TRY IT OUT

UNDER-THE-HOOD MATHEMATICS

Still not convinced that math is a must for a good mechanic? Grab your calculator and copies of the following books for some fuel for thought.

Lawler, John. *Auto Math Handbook: Calculations, Formulas, Equations, and Theory for Automotive Enthusiasts.* Los Angeles: H.P. Books, 1991.

Moore, George, Larry Sformo, and Todd Sformo. *Practical Problems in Mathematics for Automotive Technicians.* Albany, N.Y.: Delmar, 1997.

And to explore other automotive career opportunities, read Michele Krebs' book *Careers Without College: Cars* (Princeton, N.J.: Peterson's Guides, 1992).

ON-LINE GOLD MINES

Here's a website you won't want to miss: http://www.innerbody.com/innerauto/htm/auto.html. The site gives auto fanatics the chance to click on any of 10 automotive systems for a detailed and animated look at how they work.

Other websites that will appeal to the mechanically inclined are

- ☼ Popular Mechanics for Kids at http://www.pm4kids.com
- ☼ Popular Mechanics at http://popularmechanics.com
- ☼ The Auto Channel at http://www.theautochannel.com
- ☼ Car Talk at http://cartalk.cars.com

AUTO ANATOMY

If you plan on fixing cars, the more you know about how they're supposed to work, the better. Find out all you can about how the various parts and systems of cars combine to keep things moving. Some books to start your search are

Cruikshank, Gordon. *DK Pockets: Cars.* New York: DK Publishing, 1996.

Cruikshank, Gordon, and Alan Austin. *Cars and How They Work.* New York: DK Publishing, 1992.

Horton, Chris, and Karl Lundvigsen. *The Encyclopedia of Cars.* Philadelphia: Chelsea House, 1997.

Johnstone, Michael, and Alan Austin. *Look Inside Cross-Sections: Cars.* New York: DK Publishers, 1995.

Royston, Angela. *The A-to-Z Book of Cars.* New York: Barron's, 1995.

Sutton, Richard. *Car: An Eyewitness Book.* New York: Knopf, 1990.

Once you've got the general idea, move on to real cars. Don't stop until you can identify every part under the hood.

HOT WHEELS

No matter what your dream cars may be, you'll find them all at http://www.supercars.net. Pick your favorites and keep a running tally on what makes each one hot.

Also, make good use of all that passenger time you spend riding around in cars. Start noticing the different makes and models of the cars and trucks that whiz by. Use the various automotive manufacturer's websites to find out all you can about the special features of each year's new editions.

MR. OR MS. FIX-IT

If you're considering a career as a mechanic, the best thing you can do is tinker around with cars (under adult supervision, of course) every chance you get. Once you get to high school, you may have the opportunity to take an automotive shop class or to enroll in a program at a cooperating vocational education school. Do it if you can.

In the meantime, you can learn about car problems, diagnosing them, and solutions to them with an easy-to-use and very informative software program called Auto Tech. The program can be ordered by calling 800-746-8013.

MOUSE ON WHEELS

Maybe you're not old enough to drive a real car yet, but who says you can't get behind the wheel of a mousetrap car? Making a mousetrap car can be a fun and challenging project. The only necessary material for the car is a mousetrap, which when sprung, will act as the "engine" of the car. It is up to you, though, to create a design that uses other materials, such as wood, pipes, string, and of course wheels. Can you make a car that travels farther or faster than others? Check out the following sites for instructions on how to make a sample mousetrap car and for plenty of ideas for what to do when you're ready to hit the road.

☼ http://www.docfizzix.com
☼ http://www.geocities.com/CapeCanaveral/5080/
   LabReport.html

Get some friends to make their own versions and have a race. May the best mouse win!

CHECK IT OUT

American Automobile Manufacturers Association
7430 Second Avenue, Suite 300
Detroit, Michigan 48202
http://www.aama.com

Automotive Service Association
1901 Airport Freeway
Bedford, Texas 76021-5732
http://www.asashop.org

Automotive Service Industry Association
25 Northwest Point
Elk Grove Village, Illinois 60007-1035

National Automotive Technicians Education Foundation
13505 Dulles Technology Drive
Herndon, Virginia 22071-3415
http://www.asecert.org

Contact the following automobile manufacturers about apprenticeship and scholarship programs for automotive service technology.

ASSET Program
Training Department
Ford Parts and Service Division
3000 Schaefer Road, Room 109
Dearborn, Michigan 48121

Chrysler Dealer Apprenticeship Program
National CAP Coordinator
CIMS 423-21-06
26001 Lawrence Avenue
Center Line, Michigan 48015
800-626-1523

General Motors Automotive Service Educational Program
National College Coordinator
General Motors Service Technology Group
30501 Van Dyke Avenue
Warren, Michigan 48090
800-828-6860

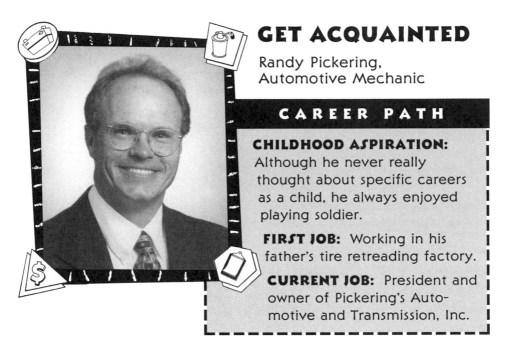

GET ACQUAINTED

Randy Pickering,
Automotive Mechanic

CAREER PATH

CHILDHOOD ASPIRATION:
Although he never really
thought about specific careers
as a child, he always enjoyed
playing soldier.

FIRST JOB: Working in his
father's tire retreading factory.

CURRENT JOB: President and
owner of Pickering's Automotive and Transmission, Inc.

A FAMILY TRADITION

Randy Pickering says that cars are in his blood. Pickering's
great-grandfather started his career as a blacksmith but, when
cars were invented, made the switch (as was common among
blacksmiths then) to become one of the first automobile
mechanics. His grandfather owned a gas station back when the
notion of self-service was unheard of and gas stations routinely provided a number of services such as pumping the gas,
checking the oil, and putting air in the tires. Next on the family tree were Pickering's father and uncle who owned a tire
retreading factory. And that's just his dad's side of the family.

Cars and tires were recurrent themes on his mom's side as
well. And both sides of the family had a penchant for racing
sports cars, so it's easy to see that automobiles were an important part of Pickering's life from the get-go.

THE TRADITION CONTINUES

Whenever Pickering's mom needed some peace and quiet
around the house, she sent her young sons to work with their

34

father. There Pickering and his big brother learned about the world of work for just 25¢ day. As youngsters, they swept floors, stacked tires, and did other types of manual labor to help their dad. As they got older, they got more involved in the retreading process.

As a teenager, Pickering can recall his father teaching him how to make sales calls and handle the office telephones. It was through this experience that Pickering discovered his natural knack for working with people.

MORE THAN ONE ROUTE TO SUCCESS

After graduating from high school, Pickering enrolled in a college not far from his home and pursued a degree in business. He eagerly signed up for a full load of college courses, went to school all morning, and raced to the factory to work all afternoon and on into the evening. The schedule didn't leave much time for studying, and it wasn't long before Pickering started falling behind in his classes.

Frustrated and not enjoying the college experience at all, Pickering jumped at the chance to take over an open sales route for his father's company. Now his schedule involved loading up a truck and trailer with retreaded tires on Monday, driving out to his territory and delivering orders to customers until Wednesday, heading back for home to reload, and then hitting the road again on Thursday. He loved the work and was soon the number one salesperson for the entire business.

Pickering worked for his father's business in various capacities for several years until he had the chance to go out on his own. By that time, he was a pretty savvy businessperson. He purchased a small automobile repair shop and managed to double the shop's sales in just one year. Business kept growing until the shop was literally bursting at the seams, and Pickering then decided it was time to create his dream company from scratch.

Looking back, Pickering says he eventually got the education he missed by dropping out of college. It took a little longer, and he may have had to work harder to learn the ropes, but he's found his own way to success.

CHEESEBURGER, FRIES, AND A FRONT-END ALIGNMENT?

Pickering's brand-new auto repair shop brings some unexpected surprises. For one thing, the typical "grease monkey" decor is replaced by a clean and enjoyable blast from the past. It's like walking into an old-fashioned soda fountain where friendly and knowledgeable service advisers are just as likely to offer you a piece of bubble gum as car repair advice. Step into the waiting room and step back in time where high-quality service and personal attention are the norm and words like *honest* and *fair* are the only buzzwords needed to describe successful businesspeople.

When it came time to expand his business in a new location, Pickering decided to add some fun to a sometimes frustrating experience. Nobody *wants* to deal with a car that doesn't work, but if you've got to, Pickering tries to make the process as enjoyable as possible.

It's a concept that's working as Pickering continues to attract both loyal customers and dedicated employees. A winning combination for any business!

Banker

WHAT IS A BANKER?

In case you haven't noticed, there's a lot of money floating around out there. Even kids like you have at least a little bit to spend—and when you put your little bit together with everyone else's little bit, that adds up to really big bucks. According to a study by Texas A&M University, in one year kids in the United States spend

- $2 billion on junk food
- $1.9 billion on toys and games
- $600 million on movies, shows, concerts, and sporting events
- $486 million on arcade video games
- $264 million on miscellaneous items such as stereos, cosmetics, and other living expenses

Now, if kids like you have that much money, just think of how much the adults with real jobs have! All that money is what keeps bankers in business. Bankers help people manage their money with savings accounts, checking accounts, credit cards, mortgage loans for houses, car loans, investment opportunities, and other types of financial services.

The banking industry as a whole offers many different kinds of career possibilities. Some specific options within the field include

mortgage banker, who works in the very specialized area of helping people secure loans for homes.

loan officer, who helps customers in need of money to buy cars, consolidate debt, or make other major purchases.

commercial banker, who works with businesses to handle their specialized banking needs.

investment banker, who manages investment portfolios for bank customers, including individuals, businesses, and governments.

trust officer, who handles special kinds of accounts called trusts, helps customers plan what to do with their money and assets after they die (called estate planning), and helps customers manage inheritance income.

Opportunities in banks vary widely according to a person's education and experience. Someone with only a high school diploma might work as a teller, a customer service representative, a data entry clerk, or an administrative assistant. A college degree in finance, economics, accounting, or business broadens the range of opportunities to include commercial or consumer loan officer, bank manager, trust officer, investment banker, financial analyst, and other more specialized jobs. As is true of any profession, the highest salaries and best perks go to those who have the jobs with the highest levels of responsibility.

In addition to working at banks similar to those you see around your community, bankers may specialize in international banking, in securities firms (such as you'd find on Wall Street), and in government entities, such as the Department of the Treasury and the Federal Reserve Board.

Successful bankers know how to work with numbers and how to deal with people. They have a firm grasp of the role money plays in our world. If you think a career in banking might be a good choice for you, start getting ready now by taking classes in math, speech, and writing to develop your communication skills, and in business and economics to find out more about the world of money.

TRY IT OUT

PRACTICE WHAT YOU PREACH

If you plan on making a career out of handling other people's money, first get a handle on your own. A basic rule of thumb in personal finance is this: For every dollar you earn, save or invest 10¢, give 10¢ away to a worthy cause, and spend the rest. To implement this plan, all you need is three containers with lids and a notebook. Label one container for each account: savings, charity, spending. Use the notebook to keep track of the cash flow (how the money is earned and what it's used for).

If you want to get fancy (and gain some expert financial advice), consider investing in the World of Allowance Kit produced by Denver-based Summit Financial Products, Inc. The kit includes a bank with three separate slots, an instruction book, an audiocassette, and a "wheel of money" that shows how invested money grows with time and interest. Look for this product in your favorite toy store or bookstore, or call 800-513-3779 for ordering information.

CYBERBANKING

You'll find all kinds of helpful information and really fun simulated banking activities on the Internet. Some sites to investigate are the following:

- 💡 http://www.kidsbank.com is where you'll find the Kids Bank website. Here you'll discover how long it will take to save a million dollars, get a chance to ask Mr. Money anything you want to know about financial matters, and visit a game room with interactive quizzes on all kinds of banking information.
- 💡 http://www.younginvestor.com/pick.shtml is a great site. Be sure to check out the game room full of fun activities such as money-tration, Wall Street trivia, brain teasers, puzzles, and more. Stop by and visit Dr. Tightwad while you're there.
- 💡 http://www.better-investing.org/youth/how-to-teach.html is a site originally intended for teachers, but since it links to all kinds of great financial websites that are appropriate for teens, it's a site you'll want to use.

PLAY MONEY

Learn more about money by gathering a couple of friends for a go-for-broke round of either of these classic Milton Bradley board games: Monopoly and Life. Or go high-tech with either of these games in a computer format produced by Hasbro Interactive. Both games provide a fun way to learn your way around the world of money. Who ends up managing their money best?

BOOKS YOU CAN BANK ON

A good banker is one who knows all about money—earning it, spending it, and saving it. Start your own financial education with any of these entertaining and very informative books.

―――――――――

Banks, Ann. *It's My Money: A Kid's Guide to the Green Stuff.* New York: Puffin Books, 1993.

Burkett, Larry, and Todd Temple. *Money Matters for Teens.* Chicago: Moody Press, 1998.

Godfrey, Neale S. *Neale S. Godfrey's Ultimate Kids' Money Book.* New York: Simon and Schuster, 1998.

Temple, Todd. *Money: How to Make It, Spend It, and Keep Lots of It.* Nashville, Tenn.: Broadman and Holman, 1998.

————————————

Take your financial education to the next level by comparing how each author advises his or her readers. Make a chart that lists each author's name, his or her best tips, and your own reaction to the author's ideas. Pick the strategy that you think sounds most reasonable, use it, and enjoy the profits.

OUT-OF-THIS-WORLD BANKING

Two incredibly fun (and free) Internet games that will test your banking skills include

- ☀ Escape from Knab at http://www.escapefromknab.com issues you a one-way ticket to the planet Knab. Once you get there, you discover that a return ticket costs $10,000. You have to get a job to earn money and save enough to buy your way back to Earth.
- ☀ Gazillionaire at http://gazillionaire.com is described as a cross between Monopoly in outer space and Wall Street in Wonderland. The game lets you head your own trading company; it challenges you to sell 100 tons of cargo (moon fern or oggle sand, anyone?) and earn 1 million "kubar" before your squid-faced competition beats you to it.

CHECK IT OUT

American Bankers Association
1120 Connecticut Avenue NW
Washington, D.C. 20036
http://www.aba.com

American Financial Services
  Association
919 18th Street NW, Suite 300
Washington, D.C. 20006

American League of Financial
  Institutions
900 19th Street NW, Suite 400
Washington, D.C. 20006
http://www.alfi.org

Financial Women International
200 North Glebe Road,
  Suite 820
Arlington, Virginia 22203-3728
http://www.fwi.org

GET ACQUAINTED

B. LaRae Orullion, Banker

CAREER PATH

CHILDHOOD ASPIRATION: To be a math or gym teacher.

FIRST JOB: Picking strawberries for 5¢ a cup and cherries for 3¢ a pound when she was a young girl.

CURRENT JOB: Vice chair, board of directors, Guaranty Bank; chair, board of directors, Frontier Airlines; chair, board of directors, BlueCross BlueShield of Colorado; and board member of several other corporations.

A LONG WAY UP

LaRae Orullion began her climb to become the first female president of a bank from the bottom rung of the banking career ladder. Her first official title at a bank in Utah was messenger girl, and her duties ranged from delivering mail to running errands at the region's federal reserve bank. The work kept her out and about in the city, and she gave it her best. Her hard work was soon rewarded with a promotion to file clerk, and she started spending her days confined to the file room in the bank's vault. Then she was promoted to coin wrapper.

Make no mistake, however. In those days, there were no fancy machines to sort and count huge piles of coins. Instead, the coin wrappers had to master the technique of balancing a roll of coins in the palms of their hands while inserting them into paper wrappers. Orullion got pretty good at it!

Throughout all these early banking jobs, Orullion was also attending banking school at night. She'd recognized that a good education was key to getting the best banking jobs. She couldn't afford to quit her job and go to school full-time, but she stuck with her schedule for 13 years until she earned 3 graduate certificates in banking. She went on to also earn a master's degree in real estate and mortgage banking.

FULL STEAM AHEAD

With a good education and lots of experience under her belt, Orullion left her hometown and headed off to make her mark on the banking world. Hoping to ultimately reach the U.S. financial center on Wall Street, she made what she assumed would be a temporary stop in Denver. There she was hired as a loan secretary, soon promoted to secretary to the president of a bank, and eventually promoted to executive vice president and director of the bank. The position made her the highest ranking woman in Denver's banking community and one of very few women at that level in the entire country.

With a successful track record like that, it's easy to understand why some of her colleagues who were starting the Women's Bank asked her to become its first president—and she accepted. The whole idea of a women's bank was a bold departure from the way things were done back in the 1970s. Experts initially scoffed at the notion of running a bank that provided equal access to services and resources; however, the naysayers settled down when Orullion and the other 50 founders of the Women's Bank bucked tradition and sold $10 million in stock simply by telling their friends and business associates about the opportunity. Those who said it couldn't be done were silenced altogether the first day the Women's Bank opened and took in $1 million in deposits and $1 million a week for the next 12 weeks. The bank even made a profit in its first month—something that takes most banks a few years to achieve!

MORE THAN ONE WAY TO NEW YORK

Needless to say, Orullion's rise to become the first female president of a bank was widely regarded as a huge success. It also became apparent that Orullion didn't have to go all the way to Wall Street to meet her highest professional ambitions. Denver has kept her plenty busy as a banker.

Nevertheless, Orullion confesses that the New York dream never completed faded. To her surprise and pleasure, she found another way to get to New York.

Strangely enough it all came about from a habit she'd developed as a teenager. Orullion has always been a tireless volunteer, and as an adult, her volunteer interests included raising funds for favorite charities and leadership positions with the Girl Scouts. All this work came together in a special way when Orullion was chosen to be president of Girl Scouts of the U.S.A. One of the perks of this volunteer position was her very own office at their national headquarters, located in New York City!

HANG IN THERE!

After all this time and all her accomplishments, Orullion still regards the advanced math courses she took in high school as some of the most important training she ever received. It was there, working on complex algebra equations, that she learned to stick with a problem until she found the solution. The mental discipline it takes to identify tough problems and work hard to solve them has been a skill that has served Orullion well as a student back then and as a bank president, community volunteer, and corporate board chairperson now.

Builder

SHORTCUTS

GO visit a construction site and observe all the work going on.

READ on-line about how to build your own house at http://www.hbrnet.hw.net.

TRY building a model airplane, birdhouse, or treehouse.

SKILL SET

✔ TALKING

✔ ADVENTURE

✔ MATH

WHAT IS A BUILDER?

As long as people need houses, roads, bridges, schools, hospitals, skyscrapers, and airports, there will be plenty of opportunities for the people who build them. Builders or carpenters are responsible for creating all of the structures found in any community—brick by brick, nail by nail. If you've ever noticed a new building going up and watched as the project grew from a hole in the ground to a sturdy structure of substance, you know what an amazing process this can be.

The work requires equal parts of physical stamina and intellectual skill. Carpenters must be adept at using many kinds of tools and must be able to read blueprints. They must be able to figure out how things go together and must be able to work with a wide variety of other building professionals.

In addition to working on buildings and other major structures, some carpenters may build furniture or specialize in remodeling homes or businesses. One of the best parts of either type of carpentry work comes from the satisfaction of a job well done. Their work makes a lasting contribution to the lives and well-being of others. It can be very gratifying to walk through a neighborhood or down a busy city street and know that your own two hands had a part in making the homes and buildings that you see.

Construction project management is another kind of work in the building industry. Project managers are essentially the boss of a construction project, and their job is to make sure that budgets are met, schedules are kept, and safety standards are followed. Construction project managers must be know-it-alls when it comes to construction. If they don't know something about plumbing, electrical wiring, standard construction techniques, blueprint reading, and the like, they won't be able to tell if the job is being done right. They gain all this experience generally from a college degree followed by several years of work in the construction industry.

Building any type of structure requires the expert workmanship of people skilled in a variety of trades. Other people involved in the construction industry include the heavy-machine operators who clear the land and dig the foundation, the roofer who puts the roof on top, and all the other tradespeople involved in the steps in between. Plumbers, iron workers, and electricians all play vital roles in the building process as well.

The type of education you'll need depends on the type of work you want to do. For someone fresh out of high school, there are opportunities to work as roofers, construction workers, electrician's helpers, and brick and mason assistants. Opportunities, salaries, and levels of job responsibility increase with more training and experience. Some of the jobs available with a two-year college associate's degree or technical certification include land surveyor, electrician, brick mason, plumber, carpenter, flooring installer, drywall installer, and heating, ventilation, and air-conditioning (HVAC) technician. With a four year degree in a field such as architecture, construction management, planning, or construction science, you would be qualified for positions that include project manager, building inspector, or estimator.

The opportunities are plentiful, and they are available for men and women alike. According to the U.S. Department of Labor, there are more than 4.84 million hands-on construction jobs performed each year in the United States. There is often more work than workers in many parts of the country. All this suggests that construction is a career you could build a future on.

TRY IT OUT

TOUR A VIRTUAL MUSEUM

Even if you don't live anywhere near Washington, D.C., you can take a virtual tour of the city's National Building Museum via the Internet at http://www.nbm.org. Here you'll find fun and informative on-line activities as well as a chance to tour some interesting exhibits. Since the museum is dedicated to exploring and celebrating architecture, design, engineering, construction, and urban planning, you are bound to learn something new. Remember as you explore the site that someone had to build all those extraordinary structures. Give yourself another 10 or 20 years, and it could be your work on exhibit!

NUTS AND BOLTS OF CONSTRUCTION

Who says you have to use hammers and nails to build things? Use the ideas featured in these books to create amazing structures made of straws, toothpicks, and balloons.

———

Pollard, J. *Building Toothpick Bridges.* White Plains, N.Y.: Dale Seymour Publications, 1985.

Zubrowski, Bernie. *Balloons: Building and Experimenting with Inflatable Toys.* New York: William Morrow, 1990.

———. *Messing Around with Drinking Straw Construction.* Boston: Little Brown, 1982.

If you insist on using hammers and nails, try these books.

Salvadori, Mario. *The Art of Construction: Projects and Principles for Beginning Engineers and Architects.* Chicago: Chicago Review Press, 1990.

Slafer, Anna. *Why Design? Activities and Projects from the National Building Museum.* Chicago: Chicago Review Press, 1995.

———

Finally, if all this constructing gets you curious about careers in the field, read Roger Sheldon's *Opportunities in Carpentry Careers* (Lincolnwood, Ill.: VGM Career Horizons, 1992).

SEE FOR YOURSELF

To find out more about the varied opportunities in the construction industry, visit the National Center for Construction Education and Research's website at http://careers.nccer.org/craft_info/career_desc.asp. Here you'll find information and on-line video demonstrations of careers such as carpenter, electrician, welder, painter, ironworker, plumber, mason, and pipefitter.

PUT YOUR HAMMER WHERE YOUR HEART IS

How does the idea of being part of a construction project and lending a helping hand sound to you? Habitat for Humanity is a nonprofit organization that builds houses for homeless people and families who cannot afford housing. Joining one of their projects can be a great way to turn a summer or spring break into a career exploration project with heart. Check your newspaper for information about local projects, or contact the organization's headquarters: Habitat for Humanity International, 121 Habitat Street, Americus, Georgia 31709.

CHECK IT OUT

Associated General Contractors of America
1957 E Street NW
Washington, D.C. 20006
http://www.agc.org

Association for Project Managers
1227 West Wrightwood Avenue
Chicago, Illinois 60614-1223
http://www.construction.st

Construction Management Association of America
7918 Jones Branch Drive, Suite 540
McLean, Virginia 22102
http://www.cmaa.org

National Association of Home Builders
1201 15th Street NW
Washington, D.C. 20005
http://www.nahb.com

National Association of Women in Construction
327 South Adams Street
Fort Worth, Texas 76104-1081
http://www.nawic.org

National Center for Construction Education and Research
P.O. Box 141104
Gainesville, Florida 32614
http://www.nccer.org

Women Construction Owners and Executives
P.O. Box 883034
San Francisco, California 94188-3034
http://www.wcoe.org

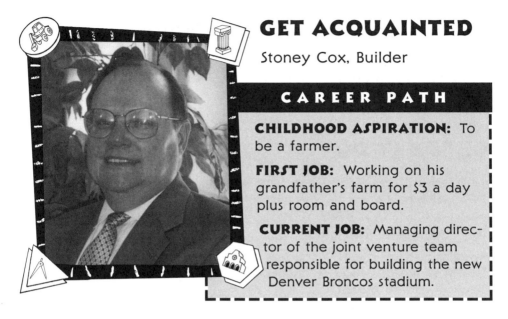

GET ACQUAINTED

Stoney Cox, Builder

CAREER PATH

CHILDHOOD ASPIRATION: To be a farmer.

FIRST JOB: Working on his grandfather's farm for $3 a day plus room and board.

CURRENT JOB: Managing director of the joint venture team responsible for building the new Denver Broncos stadium.

CLUES AND MISCUES

Stoney Cox was born on a farm and grew up assuming he'd be a farmer like his father and grandfather. About the time he started high school, though, he started considering some new ideas. Some of his relatives suggested that he become a lawyer. A guidance counselor thought he'd make a good engineer, which is the major he eventually decided to pursue in college.

Looking back, Cox says engineering was a natural choice for him. The clues were there all along. As a kid when it was time for him to do his farm chores, he could generally be found doing one of two things: either playing with his cars and trucks or playing with his Erector set (the equivalent of LEGOs in his day). His work as an adult has sometimes been a grown-up version of those childhood pastimes.

TIMING IS EVERYTHING

Cox went to college and studied to become a highway engineer. He was awarded a master's degree in civil engineering just two weeks before he was drafted into the army during the Vietnam War. Becoming a soldier was not exactly what Cox had in mind, but he decided to make the most of the situation. His college degree qualified him to apply for Officer Candidate School, which he completed to become a second lieutenant. The army wisely decided to take advantage of his education and expertise by assigning Cox to the Corps of Engineers.

UNCLE SAM NEEDS YOU!
As it turns out, the military was good for Cox—so good, that he stayed with it for 28 years. And, even though it was the Vietnam War that brought him into the military in the first place, it wasn't until 20 years later, in the Gulf War, that Cox actually fought. In addition to Iraq, Cox's military experience took him around the world to posts in Germany, Puerto Rico, Saudi Arabia, as well as throughout the United States.

Engineering wasn't the only thing he learned while in the military. Leadership, project management, people management, and teaching were other skills he picked up along the way.

A SECOND CAREER
After 28 years in the military, Cox says he decided it was time to move on. Too young to retire, he started looking for a civilian job that would make the most of all his experience. He was hired by Turner Construction, the largest building company in America. The company puts up all kinds of buildings—including hospitals, schools, prisons, skyscrapers, and laboratories.

When Cox was hired, the company gave him a few months to learn the ropes and then assigned him a whopper of a project: building a new football stadium for the two-time Super Bowl champion Denver Broncos.

TOUCHDOWN!
Cox's job as managing director of the Broncos project puts all his skills to good use. He works as liaison with the project's

architectural partner to ensure that the stadium design works in all the ways it's meant to work—in other words, that the Broncos have the space they need to practice and play football, the fans have a safe and comfortable space to enjoy the game, and the people of metropolitan Denver have a space to conduct other kinds of events during the off-season. It's a tall order, so Cox's engineering background has come in mighty handy.

In addition to building a major sports complex by a given deadline, Cox's job is to make sure that everything is done right. More than 60 architects, designers, and support people have been involved in the design process. Just estimating how much it would cost to buy all the supplies and services needed to construct the building took 6 months and a team of 15 to 20 people. Considering all the construction workers, electricians, plumbers, welders, and vendors it will take to complete the structure, Cox says the most important ingredient in his job is teamwork.

Computer Consultant

SKILL SET

✔ COMPUTERS

✔ MATH

✔ BUSINESS

GO to a computer superstore and see what's new in the world of technology.

READ *PC World* magazine (published by ZDNet). You can pick up a copy at your local newsstand or order on-line at http://www.zdnet.com/pcmag.

TRY investigating a new Internet site every day for a week.

WHAT IS A COMPUTER CONSULTANT?

Can you think of any industry that does not use computers in one way or another? Didn't think so. That's why computer consultants are in such big demand. Computers have changed virtually every type of business. Everybody's using computers, but not everybody knows how to make computers do what the person needs them to do.

Computer consultants are the "knights in shining armor" of the computer industry. They are experts in various types of computer knowledge, and they share their knowledge with others—for a fee. Computer consultants may specialize in one or more areas of computer work. Among the areas of specialization are the following:

Computer programmer, who writes instructions (called code in cyber-lingo) that tell computers what to do. Some programmers write code that tells a computer how to "talk" to its hardware. Others write code that tells the computers how to run specific programs, such as word processing or payroll. Computer consultants who specialize in programming often work within a certain kind of industry, for example, health care or banking.

53

Programmers use one or more computer languages such as BASIC, COBOL, FORTRAN, or C++ to do their work.

Computer network administrator, who installs software and sets up computer network systems. These systems can be as simple as a three-computer network in a small business or as complex as a thousand-computer system used to run a government agency in a foreign country.

Computer systems analyst, who helps clients determine which types of software and hardware best fit their company needs. This may require designing completely new computer applications or upgrading old systems. Technology changes rapidly, and a systems analyst has to be up on the latest trends in order respond to a client's needs.

Software developer, who creates and produces commercial computer software products. A software developer may be hired by a computer game company to help develop a new computer game or by a company to write programs to help a certain type of business function more effectively. For instance, a software developer might write a program for an airline to better manage its ticket reservations system, or he or she might develop a database program for a government agency to keep track of massive amounts of information.

Whatever their area of specialization, computer consultants generally work in one of two ways. Some computer consultants are self-employed with their computer knowledge being the service that their business sells. Other computer consultants work for consulting firms, which assign the consultants to projects that match their skills.

The self-employed route tends to pay more because there's no company taking a cut of the pay, but it also requires more attention to the details of running a business. Tasks such as landing the next big contract, meeting with clients, bookkeeping, and other administrative responsibilities take time away from billable hours.

Working for a consulting company offers the stability of a regular paycheck even when the consultant finishes one project and is waiting for another one to begin. It's more like a traditional 9-to-5 job and comes with all the usual health benefits, vacation time, and other perks.

Working with computers at this level requires a strong background in computer science. A college degree in computer science or information technology is a good starting point. If any type of computer career is your choice, be prepared for constant change. Some of today's hottest computer careers may be obsolete tomorrow. Smart computer consultants are always learning and upgrading so that they stay on top of emerging technology. Whether you want to write software or design computer systems, there's bound to be plenty of opportunity for computer whizzes well into the 21st century.

TRY IT OUT

LEARN THE LINGO
Computer programming is one route to a career as a computer consultant. Logo, a programming language for kids, gives you a chance to try on this career hat and see if it fits. It's easy to learn and will give you a glimpse of what it's like to boss computers around with code.

A number of versions of Logo are available, and you can download some of them from the Internet for free. Try these sites to get a copy of Logo.

- ☼ The Kids and Computers Pages at http://www.magma. ca/~dsleeth
- ☼ Softronics/MSWLogo at http://www.softronix.com
- ☼ The Great Logo Adventure at http://members.home. net/tgla

COMPUTER AEROBICS

Try out your computer skills via the activities in these books.

Colombo, Luann, and Conn McQuinn. *Fun with Computer Electronics: Build 20 Electronic Projects with the Same Type of Chips Used Inside Computers.* Kansas City, Mo.: Andrews and McMeel, 1996.

Doherty, Gillian, and Philippa Wingate. *101 Things to Do with Your Computer.* Tulsa, Okla.: EDC Publications, 1998.

Saltveit, Elin Kordahl. *Computer Fun for Everyone. Great Things to Do and Make with Any Computer.* New York: John Wiley and Sons, 1998.

Wallace, Mark. *101 Things to Do on the Internet.* Tulsa, Okla.: EDC Publishing, 1999.

If you're new to computers, you can teach yourself the basic moves with these books.

Kalman, Bobbie D. *The Computer from A to Z.* New York: Crabtree Publications, 1998.

Stephens, Margaret, and Rebecca Treays. *Computers for Beginners.* Tulsa, Okla.: EDC Publications, 1998.

If you have even the slightest inkling that you may want to pursue a career in computers, start using a computer as much as possible. Use it to do homework. Use it to play games. Use it to send e-mail to friends. Use it to explore Internet sites. The more you use it, the more you'll learn about it and the more ready you'll be to tackle some of the computer challenges that your generation will face.

COMPUTER GEEKS: PAST

Computers are amazing, and so are the people who made them happen. To get a full appreciation of all that computers do and may be able to do in the future, learn as much as you can about the history of computers. Use these websites and books (and others that you find on your own) to compile a time line illustrating computers from way back when to now.

For links to several computer history websites go to http://acusd.edu/History/classes/media/computers/historyof-computers.html.

And here are some books to look for.

The Age of Computers. Young Scientist series. Chicago: World Book Inc., 1996.

Jorberg, Charles A. *The First Computers.* Minneapolis: Abdo and Daughters, 1997.

Northrup, Mary. *American Computer Pioneers.* Springfield, N.J.: Enslow Publishers, 1998.

Parker, Steve. *Computers.* Austin, Tex.: Raintree Steck-Vaughn, 1997.

COMPUTER GEEKS: PRESENT

Find out more about the big names behind computers today. Use an Internet search engine or a library catalog to look for information about leaders in the computer industry. Some names you may want to investigate include Bill Gates, Steven Jobs, Peter Norton, Larry Ellison, and Marc Andreessen.

See if you can find out what they were like when they were your age and if any clues were evident about what their futures in computers. For instance, did they spend all their free time playing computer games? Were they exceptionally bright students? Try to find connections between your interests and theirs.

COMPUTER GEEKS: FUTURE

Now it's your turn. You are a potential computer geek of tomorrow. With the way technology keeps changing, who

knows what the future holds for tomorrow's computer professionals? Imagine what it could be like or what you hope it
will be like. Will computers be smarter than people? Will
robots take over the world? Write down your thoughts and
predictions.

CONDUCT A COMPUTER CAREER INVESTIGATION

These books provide information about a wide range of computer careers. Use them to compare the options and then
narrow them down to a list of three choices that sound good
for you.

Eberts, Marjorie, and Margaret Gisler. *Careers for Computer
Buffs and Other Technological Types.* Lincolnwood, Ill.: VGM
Career Horizons, 1996.

Hawkins, Lori, and Betsy Dowling. *100 Jobs in Technology.*
New York: Macmillan, 1996.

Morgan, Bradley J., and Joseph M. Palmisano. *Computer and
Software Design Career Directory.* Detroit: Gale Research, 1993.

Reeves, Diane Lindsey, and Peter Kent. *Career Ideas for Kids
Who Like Computers.* New York: Facts On File, 1998.

Rush, Janet. *Computer Consultants Guide.* New York: John
Wiley and Sons, 1994.

Weigant, Chris. *Choosing a Career in Computers.* New York:
Rosen Publishing, 1996.

Williams, Linda. *Careers Without College: Computers.*
Princeton, N.J.: Peterson's Guides, 1992.

CHECK IT OUT

Association for Computing Machinery
1516 Broadway
New York, New York 10036
http://www.acm.org

Association of Information Technology Professionals
505 Busse Highway
Park Ridge, Illinois 60068
http://www.aitp.org

Information Technology Association of America
1616 North Fort Meyer Drive, Suite 1300
Arlington, Virginia 22209
http://www.itaa.org

Institute of Electrical and Electronics Engineers
345 East 47th Street
New York, New York 10017
http://www.ieee.org

International Computer Consultants Association
11131 South Towne Square, Suite F
St. Louis, Missouri 63123
http://www.icca.org

National Association of Computer Consultant Businesses
715 North Eugene Street
Greensboro, North Carolina 27401
http://www.naccb.org

National Association of Programmers
P.O. Box 529
Prairieville, Louisiana 70769

GET ACQUAINTED

Garon Reeves,
Computer Consultant

CAREER PATH

CHILDHOOD ASPIRATION: To be president of the United States.

FIRST JOB: Washing dishes in a restaurant.

CURRENT JOB: Self-employed computer programmer.

SNEAK ATTACK

A career in computers sort of sneaked up on Garon Reeves. His first encounter with computers was in high school with a terminal attached to a local company's mainframe computer. The terminal didn't even have a screen. It just printed out on paper.

Reeves took a basic programming class in college at the United States Military Academy. Reeves recalls catching on fast and enjoying it, but he was so eager to be an infantry officer that he didn't take much notice at the time. He wound up majoring in Chinese language instead.

His next encounter with computers came in the wee hours of the night when it was his turn to serve as duty officer for his battalion at Schofield Barracks in Hawaii. In order to stay awake for the 24-hour shift, Reeves would fool around with the battalion's IBM word processor. He soon knew more about it than the clerks who used it every day did. It didn't take long before word got out that Reeves was the resident computer expert.

After spending several years in the military, Reeves resigned to pursue a master's degree in geology. Having married and had two children, Reeves needed a way to help support his family while he completed his studies. He was hired as a computer assistant in the school's computer lab where he had to stay two steps ahead of the other students in order to answer their computer questions. He learned a lot about computers while he was there. Probably the most important lesson he learned was that he liked computers better than he liked rocks.

THE WIZARD OF DOS

Instead of using his hard-won geology degree in the oil industry as many of his classmates did, Reeves decided to use his natural affinity with computers to start a business called Wizard of DOS. The business focused on helping small businesses with their computer systems. Troubleshooting and fixing all kinds of computer software problems was a big part of the job.

Reeves credits his success in the business to a mixture of computer know-how and an ability to relate well to his clients— a trait that's often missing in professionals with high-tech minds. Sure, Reeves was a computer geek, but that didn't mean that his clients couldn't talk to him. He had the uncanny ability to explain even the most complex computer processes in a way that his clients could understand.

BIGGER FISH TO FRY

Over several years, Reeves built up a loyal base of customers but eventually sold the business in order to expand his horizons in the computer profession. He started looking for long-term computer programming projects and found his first big gig with a team assigned the daunting task of automating the U.S. Navy's massive personnel and payroll systems. The project took him away from home a lot for an entire year while he commuted between New Orleans and Denver. The experience paid off; when he finished up, he landed another big project helping to revamp a public school system's personnel and payroll systems at twice the pay.

DON'T TRY THIS AT HOME

Reeves is a bit unusual in that he is a self-taught computer whiz. His engineering and geology background certainly helped train his mind for the logic and high-level mathematics required in programming, but Reeves has never had any "official" computer training beyond that first programming class at West Point.

He would not recommend this route for everyone, but it's one that's worked for him. Reeves says an ability to learn fast and think on your feet are probably some of the best skills a computer consultant can possess. Technology changes so quickly that colleges and trade schools can barely keep up. You have to be a self-motivated learner to stay on top of the game.

Economist

WHAT IS AN ECONOMIST?

An economist is a social scientist who solves the mysteries of how people and society operate. An economist looks at why people do what they do, especially in terms of their resources, such as time, money, and material goods. An economist is guided by, and may even come up with, economic theories, such as supply and demand, and other more mundane nuggets of wisdom, such as "there's no such thing as a free lunch."

Some of the issues economists commonly deal with include international food supply, job opportunities, the banking system, health care services, urban community development, poverty, AIDS (acquired immunodeficiency syndrome) and other health concerns, corporate finance, international competition, and public utilities. But people with a strong background in economics are prepared to work in all kinds of professions, not just as an economist. Here are a few job titles you might aspire to: economic forecaster, international economist, investment banker, federal reserve bank officer, Bureau of Labor Statistics analyst, Federal Trade Commission commissioner, foreign service executive, business analyst, labor negotiator, and contract administrator.

To get started in an economics career, you'll need at least a bachelor's degree in economics. This major will focus on problem-solving skills and will require courses such as statistics, calculus, and computer science, which require strong math skills. It will also focus on economic principles based in history and social science. Economics can be a very challenging academic program, but it's one that is well regarded and one that provides the winning ticket for a number of career choices.

An economics major in college could be a good choice for you if you are interested in a career in bank management, business, labor relations, operations analysis, or a management-level position in a government agency or corporation. Economists work in all aspects of business including manufacturing, mining, banking, insurance, and retailing. There are also opportunities in the sports, recreation, entertainment, and technology industries. And while economics provides many interesting career options in and of itself, it can also be used as a springboard to go into fields such as law, politics, and business.

Although there are no guarantees, evidence does support the idea that those employed in an economics-related profession tend to earn significantly more money than the national average. According to the Bureau of Labor Statistics, a bachelor's degree in economics was one of the top five degrees for

high earning power, with men over 30 making an average of $50,360 each year. Another survey conducted by the National Association of Business Economists found that the average salary for business economists was $70,000.

TRY IT OUT

ECONOMIC FUN AND GAMES

If you feel a little intimidated about the idea of an economics career, there are a few websites that will let you wade your way into some important economic principles and have a little fun at the same time.

First, try out Ken White's Coin Flipping Page (http://shazam.econ.ubc.ca/flip). Here you can test your skills in probability and statistics.

Go in a little deeper with The Election Calculator (http://www.mit.edu/people/irons/myjava/ecalc.html). Here you can enter your forecasts about the future of the economy and predict past and future presidential elections.

Now, if you are ready to jump in with both feet, go to The National Budget Simulation (http://garnet.berkeley.edu:3333/budget/budget.html), where you'll have a chance to balance the national budget. Start with the short version of the game to learn the basics. Once you get the hang of it, move on to the long version where you'll get into some of the nitty-gritty details of economics.

AN ECONOMIC TREASURE HUNT

Visit the Federal Reserve Bank of San Francisco's economic treasure hunt and dig for gold in this fun and (dare we admit it?) educational website. Start the hunt at http://www.frbsf.org/econedu/curriculum/treshunt/beginhunt2.html. If you need help with the clues, you'll find all kinds of information about great economists and their times at http://www.frbsf.org/econedu/unfrmd.great/greattimes.html.

TOYS FOR EVERYONE

If you are interested in a career in business economics, the following activity will give you an idea of the type of work you might do. Pretend that you are president of an international toy company. Your latest gizmo is selling so well in the United States that you want to expand into other countries' markets. Pick a country where you want to start and answer the following questions.

- ☼ Where is the country?
- ☼ How large is it (in population, national income, and geographic size) compared to the United States?
- ☼ How many children under the age of 12 live there?
- ☼ How much money do most of the adults earn each year?

To find answers to your questions use the CIA's *World Factbook,* which can be consulted on-line at http://www.odci.gov/cia/publications/factbook/index.html. Another good source of information about communities around the world is http://city.net, where you can search your country.

You may want to ask a parent or teacher to help you find these answers. Once you have, write up a brief report with your recommendation of whether or not the country would be a good market for your toys.

ECONOMIC DETECTIVE

Travel the world while tracking down the infamous and elusive Gang of 15 at this fun website: http://ecedweb.unomaha.edu/gang1.htm. While you're solving the mystery, you'll learn about the currencies of other countries and exchange rates and get a taste of international economics.

GLOBAL GROCERIES

Join students from other countries on a global grocery shopping spree at http://www.landmark-project.com/ggl.html. Pick a favorite food and compare prices with students from all over the world. This Landmark Project website has been active since 1987, so there is plenty of information for you to compute, analyze, and discuss—just like a real international economist!

THE WELL-READ ECONOMIST
If books are your preferred method of learning, here's a list to begin your economic education.

Bungum, Jane E. *Money and Financial Institutions.* Minneapolis: Lerner Publications, 1991.

Clawson, Elmer. *Activities and Investigations in Economics.* New York: Addison-Wesley, 1994.

Lubov, Andrea, and M. Barbara Killen. *Taxes and Government Spending.* Minneapolis: Lerner Publications, 1990.

O'Toole, Thomas. *Global Economics.* Minneapolis: Lerner Publications, 1991.

Walz, Michael K., and M. Barbara Killen. *The Law and Economics: Your Rights as a Consumer.* Minneapolis: Lerner Publications, 1990.

CHECK IT OUT

American Economic Association
2014 Broadway, Suite 305
Nashville, Tennessee 37203
http://www.vanderbilt.edu/AEA/org.htm

National Association for Business Economists
1233 20th Street NW, Suite 505
Washington, D.C. 20036
http://www.nabe.com

National Council on Economic Education
1140 Avenue of the Americas
New York, New York 10036
http://www.nationalcouncil.org

National Economic Association
c/o Urban Institute
2100 M Street NW
Washington, D.C. 20037
http://www.ncat.edu/~neconasc

Western Economic Association International
7400 Center Avenue, Suite 109
Huntington Beach, California 92647
http://www.weainternational.org

GET ACQUAINTED

Henk-Jan Brinkman,
Economist

CAREER PATH

CHILDHOOD ASPIRATION: To be a police officer.

FIRST JOB: Working for his neighbor's construction company.

CURRENT JOB: Economic affairs officer, United Nations.

PLAN B

Henk-Jan Brinkman grew up in the Netherlands. By the time he got into high school, he was gearing up to follow in his father's footsteps as an engineer. That plan took an unexpected turn when he failed the final exam in high school and had to repeat his final year.

Given a year to reevaluate his career choice, Brinkman started asking his teachers for advice. One teacher suggested that if he wanted to make good money, he should study economics. Before long, Brinkman started looking into that profession. The more he found out about economics, the more he liked it. Like engineering, economics combined the study of math and science. But as a social science, it also added a human element. Brinkman found that at its very root, economics was all about improving the standard of living for people. This aspect appealed to Brinkman because he felt it would give him a chance to make a difference.

Looking back, Brinkman realizes how different his life would have been if he had passed that exam and become an engineer. He can honestly say, however, that he's very happy with the way things turned out.

A MAN WITHOUT A COUNTRY

After graduating from high school, Brinkman started his college education at the University of Groningen in the Netherlands. Doctoral economic studies brought him to the United States, where he studied at the New School for Social Research in New York and started working for the United Nations. He now works as a development economist specializing in Africa.

In order to work for the United Nations, Brinkman had to sign a contract promising that his allegiance would be to the world and not to any particular country. Even though the Netherlands is his homeland and the United States is where he is raising his own child, he has promised to work for the international common good.

ALL IN A DAY'S WORK

A typical day for Brinkman involves three types of activities. First, Brinkman spends some time reading newspapers, reports, and other resources and visiting Internet sites to find out what's happening in the world.

Second, Brinkman takes all the data and information that he acquires and analyzes what he's learned. Sometimes this means putting seemingly unrelated events together to determine their combined impact on a situation. For instance, the unusual El Niño weather patterns in 1997 and 1998 played an important role in economics around the world. Drought, hurricanes, and other weather-related catastrophes can have a major impact on entire nations. Studying and thinking through such issues allows economists like Brinkman to recognize and address problems and provide recommendations so that governments can make the most out of bad situations, especially *before* they happen.

Another part of this process might involve "what if" simulations. Brinkman has to imagine various situations and analyze how they would impact Africa. What if the stock market were to crash? What if there was a major oil embargo? What if the Asian nations were to suffer a major recession? What if prices of cocoa and coffee were to fall? Brinkman and his colleagues use a very powerful economic computer program called Project Link to help analyze these types of scenarios. This program is a huge model of the world economy that links individual countries to each other. It helps them determine the cause and effect of all kinds of global issues.

The third part of Brinkman's work involves writing reports. Every month, he must submit to the secretary general of the United Nations a report detailing the current happenings and any major economic developments in Africa. He's also responsible for writing about special issues such as developing nations that have debt they can't repay. A big project that Brinkman works on each year is the *World Economic and Social Survey.* This major report is used by the United Nations to identify and address international social and economic issues. To see samples of the kinds of reports Brinkman writes, visit the U.N.'s website (http://www.un.org/esa).

ECONOMICS AND YOU

If you think a career in economics might be a good choice for you, Brinkman suggests you take classes in both math and social sciences. Read newspapers and know what's happening in other parts of the world. Curiosity is one of the best assets an economist can possess.

Geographer

SHORTCUTS

GO to the library, compare a current world atlas with one that was published 10 years ago, and see if you can find at least 3 "new" countries.

READ *National Geographic* magazine.

TRY finding all the states on a U.S. map and naming each state capital.

WHAT IS A GEOGRAPHER?

A geographer is a scientist who deals with the earth and its life—especially the description of the land, sea, and air, and the distribution of plant and animal life, including humans and their industries—with reference to the mutual relations of these diverse elements. Hmmm . . . that's a mouth full. Essentially it boils down to this: Geographers study places and people and how the two interact with each other.

According to the Association of American Geographers, you can get a good idea if you'd like working as a geographer by taking this Is Geography for Me? quiz.

- ☀ Are you curious about places?
- ☀ Do you like to study maps?
- ☀ Do you prefer the window seat on airplanes?
- ☀ Are you interested in foreign areas?
- ☀ Do you like to work outside?
- ☀ Are you a problem solver?
- ☀ Are you good at seeing connections among seemingly unrelated processes?
- ☀ Can you adapt to rapid technological change?
- ☀ Do you try to see the big picture?
- ☀ Are you interested in the connections between humans and the environment?

If you answer yes to most of these questions, you may want to give a career in geography serious consideration. As a geographer, there are many different ways to apply your skills. For example, regional geographers become experts in major regions of the world, such as the Middle East or Europe, and may work for a government agency or in international business.

Environmental geographers focus on how humans use the earth, They might specialize in areas such as toxic waste, air pollution, and energy issues. Some of the places these geographers might work include a national park, a state department of environmental protection, or the federal Environmental Protection Agency.

Economic geography is another area of specialization for geographers. This area focuses on issues such as industry, business, transportation, trade, and the changing value of real estate. You'll find economic geographers employed by many types of companies, especially those that do business in more than one country. They work in marketing firms and in large real estate companies and banks. They also serve as traffic managers for companies that must ship their goods to lots of places.

Two of the most rapidly growing areas of geographic work involve cartography and geographic information systems (GIS). Cartography is the science of making maps, and GIS are highly sophisticated computer programs that can store, display, analyze, and map information. Geographers who specialize in cartography or GIS might work for government agencies such as the Census Bureau or the U.S. Geological Survey, or they might be employed by businesses such as telephone companies or real estate developers.

While geographers need a well-rounded educational background and a college degree in geography, they should also prepare themselves for specific demands. For instance, a regional geographer will probably need to be fluent in a second language, while a cartographer will need well-developed computer skills.

Earning a college degree in geography is a great way to open doors to all kinds of opportunities. Don't be surprised, however, to find out that few professionals who practice geography are actually called geographers. Instead, depending on their area of specialization, job titles might include area specialist, cartographer, environmental manager, and zoning inspector. So, if you aced the Is Geography for Me? quiz, you still need to explore the many ways you can make geography an exciting part of your career.

TRY IT OUT

MATT'S TOP TEN

To see more of the world than you ever dreamed possible, all you need is a computer with a connection to the Internet. Start your worldwide globe-trotting at the following award-winning top-10 websites chosen by the Mining Company's in-the-know geography guide, Matt Rosenberg (see interview on page 77).

- ☀ At Map Quest (http://www.mapquest.com) you'll find directions to drive from your town to any place in the United States.
- ☀ Microsoft Expedia Maps (http://www.expediamaps.com) offers good-looking area maps of anywhere on Earth.

- The on-line CIA World Factbook (http://www.odci.gov/cia/publications/factbook/ref.html) provides a great source of geographic, economic, political, and cultural information about almost every country in the world.
- Map Machine (http://www.nationalgeographic.com/maps/index.html) includes maps and geographic information about the world's countries; U.S. state, political, and physical maps of each continent; and beautiful satellite map images of the world.
- Terra Server (http://terraserver.microsoft.com) is the best, and perhaps the only, place to see a photo of your house from space.
- Perry-Castañeda Library Map Collection (http://www.lib.utexas.edu./Libs/PCL/Map_collection/Map_collection.html) holds hundreds of world maps.
- International Data Base Summary Demographic Data (http://www.census.gov/ipc/www/idbsum.html) is one of the best sources for current information about the population in various countries.
- At World Climate (http://www.worldclimate.com) you can check the weather for your own hometown and any other spot in the world.
- The Library of Congress Country Studies (http://lcwweb2.loc.gov/frd/cs/cshome.html) includes 85 full-length books that provide some of the most detailed and informative resources available on-line.
- Flags of the World (http://fotw.digibel.be/flags/) has images of more than 2,700 flags and offers a chance to learn about the geopolitical history of each place represented by a flag.

If you're still eager for more information about geography after visiting these sites, try some of the following for links to an incredible array of information, activities, and lots of fun and games.

- The Mining Company (http://geography.miningco.com) provides an up-to-date on-line newsletter with links to interesting geography sites.

☼ McREL (http://www.mcrel.org/resources/links/geo.asp) provides an exhaustive list of geography links.

☼ Geography World (http://members.aol.com/bowermanb/101.html) shows the way to dozens of geography games.

TODAY'S LESSON IS . . .

According to the National Council for Geographic Education and the Association of American Geographers, the study of geography (and the work of geographers) can be summed up in five themes. Following are brief descriptions of each theme along with an "assignment" for putting each theme to use.

1. **Location:** No matter where you are on Earth, that spot is marked by an imaginary grid of lines called latitude and longitude. Geographers use longitude and latitude to communicate precisely and accurately where a particular place is located.

   Put this theme to work by using a map to find the latitude and longitude of the place where you live. See if you can also find the spot on Earth that is exactly opposite from your location.

2. **Place:** In order to paint verbal pictures of a particular place, geographers describe them by their physical and human characteristics. These characteristics might include language, religion, and the types of work available, as well as the surrounding landscape and the surrounding buildings.

   Put this theme to work by describing the "place" surrounding your school. Make a list of all the characteristics that make it unique and compare it with a list describing a rival school across town or nearby.

3. **Human and Environmental Interaction:** In order to plan and manage the environment wisely, geographers study the ways in which humans interact with their environment.

   Put this theme to work by talking to someone who has lived in your area for 25 years or more and ask them to describe how things have changed over the years.

4. **Movement:** All people are in connection with, and dependent on, other regions, cultures, and people in the world. Interaction among all kinds of people takes place every day as people travel, communicate with one another, and rely on one another for products, information, and ideas.

   Put this theme to work by using the yellow pages in the phone book to look up restaurants. Make a list of all the different kinds of ethnic groups represented by the various restaurants. At the very least, your list should include Chinese, Mexican, and Italian. Choose one country and use an encyclopedia to find out all you can about it. Try to find some connection between the country and the type of food it is known for. For instance, if rice is known as a main staple of the cuisine, is it also known as a major export for that country?

5. **Regions:** Regions are areas in the world that are defined by certain unifying physical, human, or cultural characteristics. Geographers study how regions change over time.

   Put this theme to work by using a map to divide the United States into regions based on your ideas about the physical, human, or cultural characteristics of the area. For instance, you might put all the states west of the Mississippi River and east of the Rocky Mountains into a region and you might put the states that border the Atlantic Ocean into another region. If it's your own map and it's OK to write on it, use a marker to indicate each region and write three words or phrases that describe each region.

For more information and activities involving these themes, visit National Geographic's geography education website at http://www.nationalgeographic.com/resources/ngo/education/themes.html.

MAPS 101

Thanks to the ingenuity of the United States Geological Survey, you can become an expert on reading and making maps via the Internet. Go to the Exploring Maps website at http://www.usgs.gov/education/learnweb/Maps.html and work your way through activities on location, navigation, information, and exploration.

ALL THE BUZZ ABOUT THE GEOGRAPHY BEE

The National Geographic Society sponsors an annual Geography Bee to get students in grades four through eight interested in geography. National winners of the Geography Bee receive college scholarships.

You'll need your school principal's help in order to participate. Principals must send in a written request on school letterhead for a registration packet and a check to National Geography Bee, National Geographic Society, 1145 17th Street NW, Washington, D.C. 20036-4688.

WONDERS TIMES SEVEN

Have you ever heard of the Seven Wonders of the World? You can get a firsthand look at both the ancient wonders and the modern versions by going to http://pharos.bu.edu/Egypt/Wonders.

While you're there, compare the lists and compile your own version based on which you think are the most spectacular. Print out pictures of each site and make a poster depicting your choices for an all-time seven wonders list. Feel free to add new locations that you think merit the distinction.

CHECK IT OUT

Association of American Geographers
1710 16th Street NW
Washington, D.C. 20009
http://www.aag.org

Center for Geographic Education
San Jose State University
San Jose, California 95192-0116
http://www.sjsu.edu/depts/cge

National Geographic Society
1145 17th Street NW
Washington, D.C. 20036-4688
http://www.nationalgeographic.com

United States Geological Survey
807 National Center
Reston, Virginia 20192
http://www.usgs.gov

GET ACQUAINTED

Matthew Rosenberg,
Geographer

CAREER PATH

CHILDHOOD ASPIRATION: To be a policeman, fireman, or reporter.

FIRST JOB: Student assistant in a university library.

CURRENT JOB: Author, web-master for an on-line geography site, and GIS technician.

A CHANGE IN PLANS

Matthew Rosenberg has always been fascinated by geography. He just didn't know it for a long time. Even as a young child, he was fascinated by maps and spent lots of time exploring his neighborhood. Sometimes he'd even sketch maps of the rural areas around his home.

The first time he encountered an official geography class was in his first year of college. When he enrolled in college, he fully intended to become a doctor. He signed up for an introduction to urban and economical geography course just to fulfill a general education requirement, so he was surprised when the class opened up a whole new world to him—literally. He'd never heard of geography as a career, let alone considered it for himself. Just one class, however, and he was hooked. He promptly changed his major to geography and ended up changing his destiny.

A JUGGLING ACT

Rosenberg loves geography. It's more than a profession to him; it's a passion. His enthusiasm for the subject is apparent in all the ways Rosenberg makes geography a part of his life. When it comes right down to it, Rosenberg wears several different geography hats.

One hat is as resident expert for a very popular geography website. Rosenberg is the geography guide for the Mining Company's geography site at http://geography.miningco.com. In this role, he spends 10 to 20 hours a week researching and writing articles about all kinds of geography-related topics. One week it could be avalanches, while another week it might be the world's political distribution. He also searches the Internet to find sites of interest to geographers and manages a geography chat room.

This role has provided all kinds of opportunities for Rosenberg. One of the nicest (and most surprising!) opportunities came when he received an e-mail message from a book editor asking him to write a book about geography. This opportunity resulted in a new geography hat for Rosenberg to wear: that of author. The challenge of writing a book was so satisfying to Rosenberg that he plans to do it again soon.

Geographic information systems (GIS) technician is another one of the hats that Rosenberg wears most days. In this role, he works for the city of Santa Clarita gathering data to make new layers of maps for the city. These maps are so specific that they might indicate where all the city's stop signs are located and where to find all the potholes. The work requires meticulous attention to space and detail.

And there's still another hat left for Rosenberg to wear: that of student. Rosenberg is currently working toward a doctorate degree in urban geography and hazards research. It makes for a busy schedule, but it is one that Rosenberg hopes will lead him to his ultimate goal of becoming a geography professor and sharing his passion for the world with others.

A FEW SUGGESTIONS

If you are considering a career in geography, Rosenberg has a few suggestions for you.

First of all, be curious. Read the newspaper and watch the news to find out what's happening in the world. Look at maps. Rosenberg says that future geographers should learn to use a world atlas the same way other people use a dictionary. When you hear about a place you aren't familiar with, look it up!

Second, be an explorer. Start noticing where you are and what it's like. Observe your environment and make observations about it. Looking is one thing, but understanding is another. Make sure you do both.

And, finally, when you get to high school, find out if your school offers an advanced placement (AP) geography course. If it does, take it and get a good introduction to what the field is all about. Plus, you'll get a chance to earn college credit while you're still in high school.

THE ANSWER MAN

Have you ever wondered who owns the oceans or which state has the most lakes? Are you intrigued by real-life geographic disasters such as the lake that killed more than 2,000 people? If so, you'll want to read Rosenberg's book *The Handy Geography Answer Book* (Detroit: Visible Ink Press, 1998). In the book, Rosenberg tackles 1,000 geography questions and provides fun and fact-filled answers to satisfy curious geography buffs.

Still have geography questions after reading the book? Rosenberg welcomes them one and all. E-mail your queries to him at geography.guide@miningco.com.

Machinist

SKILL SET

✔ MATH
✔ COMPUTERS
✔ ADVENTURE

WHAT IS A MACHINIST?

A machinist makes the plastic and metal components that are part of products you use every day. Toothbrushes, skateboard wheels, car parts, plumbing pipes, and computer keyboards are just a few examples of a machinist's magic.

To do their jobs, machinists use different kinds of machines and tools, including lathes, milling machines, surface grinders, and drill presses. They work with a wide variety of materials including such metals as steel, cast iron, aluminum, and brass and other materials such as plastics or ceramics.

These days, many machines are controlled by computers and require machinists to read and calculate precise measurements. This work leaves little room for mistakes. Computers help get the job done right and more efficiently.

Those who are cut out for this type of work would be able to answer yes to at least several of the following questions.

💡 Are you mechanically inclined?
💡 Are you curious about the way things work?
💡 Do you like using your hands to make things?

- ☼ Do you like to fix things or take them apart and put them together again?
- ☼ Do you like using your mind in challenging, creative ways?

While machinists make parts and components for products, tool-and-die makers make the special tools and molds (called dies) needed by machinists to make the parts. Due to its complex nature, tool-and-die making is considered a step up from machining. Tool-and-die makers use many types of machine tools and precision-measurement instruments, so they have to know more about machining, mathematics, and blueprint reading than machinists generally need to know.

Other specialized career options in this field include draftsperson, metallurgist, quality control inspector, custom machine builder, welder, and instrument maker.

High school shop classes provide a head start for those interested in pursuing any type of machining career. To get the best preparation, most machinists complete a one- to two-year vocational training program that includes such classes as machining tool operations, plane geometry, trigonometry, and blueprint reading.

There are also many opportunities for on-the-job apprenticeships in which you can combine working and learning. An employer often pays an apprentice for the training, so you can earn while you learn. And as you gain skill as a machinist or tool-and-die maker, you will be able to find more jobs as a qualified technician.

TRY IT OUT

FACTS AT YOUR FINGERTIPS

If the whole idea of tool-and-die making still has you scratching your head in confusion, here's a website with pictures that show you what the process is like: http://www.brunkindustries.com.

Two other sites that are packed with information about machining are

☼ Modern Machine Shop at http://www.mmsonline.com
☼ Machinists' Exchange at http://www.machinist.net

METALWORKING 101

If you are considering a career working with machines, you should start by taking shop classes in high school. If your school does not offer shop classes, check into trade or vocational training schools in your area.

In addition to what you'll learn at school, you can set up shop at home. Before you do, however, please note that all the activities suggested below must be completed under the supervision of a trusted adult—a parent, teacher, or family friend. Do not even attempt to work with tools and metalworking equipment without adult help!

With those important instructions understood, here are a few websites that include ideas and plans for a variety of metalworking projects.

☼ Home Metal Shop Club at http://web.wt.net/%7Ehmsc/index.htm
☼ Stan's Metal Shop Project Page at http://members.xoom.com/cotreau/project.html
☼ John's Metalworking sites at http://aviator.cwis.siu.edu/john/metalsites.html.

THE SECRET LIVES OF STUFF

The How Stuff Works website is one not to be missed. It gives you the inside scoop on everything from engines and motors to televisions and cell phones. Plus it provides detailed and easy-to-read information all kinds of other stuff. Find it all at http://www.howstuffworks.com.

READ ALL ABOUT IT

If machines are to be the tools of your trade, you'll want to know everything there is to know about them. Following are some suggested reading books.

Butterfield, Moir, and Hans Jenssen. *Look Inside Cross-Sections: Record Breakers.* New York: DK Publishing, 1995.
Kirkwood, Jon. *The Fantastic Cutaway Book of Giant Machines.* Brookfield, Conn.: Millbrook Books, 1996.
Macaulay, David. *The New Way Things Work.* New York: Houghton Mifflin, 1998.
Rawson, Christopher. *How Machines Work.* Tulsa, Okla: EDC Publications, 1983.
Weaver, Rebecca. *Machines in the Home.* New York: Oxford University Press, 1992.

For more information about career options with machines, try some of these titles.

Dudzinski, George A. *Opportunities in Tool and Die Careers.* Lincolnwood, Ill.: VGM Career Horizons, 1993.
Garvey, Lonny D. *Opportunities in the Machine Trades.* Lincolnwood, Ill.: VGM Career Horizons, 1994.

A NEW TAKE ON TOOLS

Use your ingenuity and test your mechanical ability by inventing or modifying a tool for the Young Inventors Awards Program. The contest is open to all students of two groups: grades 3–5 and grades 6–8. To be eligible, you must, with the help of a teacher, parent, or other trusted adult, design and build a tool that mends, makes life easier or safer in some way, entertains, or solves an everyday problem.

For information, write to the Craftsman/NSTA Young Inventors Awards Program, National Science Teachers Association, 1840 Wilson Boulevard, Arlington, Virginia 22201-3000. You can also call 888-494-4994 or go on-line at http://www.nsta.org/programs/craftsman.htm.

PARTS AND PIECES EVERYWHERE YOU LOOK

Follow this three-step process to get an idea of how big and diverse the machining industry is.

First, make a list of all the metal and plastic parts you can find in your family's house and car. Check in the kitchen, the bathroom, under the hood, and in the passenger area. Look everywhere and list every single little piece you can find. If you don't know a part's official name, make up your own.

Second, pick one or more items from your list and make a sketch of it. Include all its details.

Third, try to figure out how the part might be made. Make a step-by-step plan of how a machinist might start with raw materials to make the finished product.

CHECK IT OUT

Association for Manufacturing Technology
7901 Westpark Drive
McLean, Virginia 22102
http://www.mfgtech.org

National Tooling and Machining Association
9300 Livingston Road
Ft. Washington, Maryland 20744-4998
http://www.ntma.org

NTMA Training Center
43651 South Grimmer Boulevard
Fremont, California 94538
http://www.ntma-sf-tc.org

Precision Machined Products Association
6700 West Snowville Road
Brecksville, Ohio 44141-3292
http://www.pmpa.org

Tooling and Manufacturing Association
1177 South Dee Road
Park Ridge, Illinois 60068
http://www.tmanet.com

GET ACQUAINTED

Maia Tedesco Dyke,
Machinist

CAREER PATH

CHILDHOOD ASPIRATION: Considered a little bit of everything from firefighter and veterinarian to engineer.

FIRST JOB: Assistant secretary at an appliance repair company.

CURRENT JOB: Tooling technician at a stamping house that specializes in making brackets, housings, and other parts for automobiles, computers, and appliances.

DOWN A NEW ROAD

Maia Tedesco Dyke says she wishes she'd had a book like this when she was still in school. She remembers feeling really lost; she didn't know what to do after she graduated. Luckily she attended a technical high school, because she had to take a shop class in order to graduate. The first shop class she took didn't do much for her, but a friend talked her into taking an advanced class the next semester. That's when things clicked. Dyke enjoyed it and was really good at it too.

Her shop teacher encouraged her to consider metalworking as a career. At first, Dyke, like many other people, thought of metalworking and machining as "men's work." Not in her wildest dreams had she ever considered it for herself. When her teacher introduced her to a woman who owned one type of metalworking business and whose husband owned another type, Dyke realized there might be more potential for women than she had previously thought.

As it turns out, it was this same woman who helped Dyke get her foot in the door. She arranged an interview for Dyke at her husband's company where Dyke was hired as a tool-and-die apprentice. Her first assignment was as an inspector involved in making sure that the parts being made at the factory were top quality. If the parts passed her inspection, Dyke would pack them up for shipping to customers.

During this time, she worked for the company during the day, and the company paid for her to go to the Tooling and Manufacturing Association's Related Theory Apprentice Training Program at night. She went to classes two nights a week for three years and studied such subjects as shop math, blueprint reading, and machining practices.

After a while she was promoted into the tool room and started learning the tool-and-die making process. Still an apprentice, she became curious about how to work the wire EDM (electrical discharge machining) system and took the initiative to learn about it—sometimes by looking over the EDM operator's shoulder and sometimes by asking questions. Her nosiness paid off when the EDM operator left the company and she got that person's job.

SO MUCH TO LEARN

If there is one thing that has marked Dyke's career, it's her constant quest for knowledge. Any time Dyke sets her sights on a new position within the company, she learns all she needs to move ahead. This process usually involves gaining on-the-job experience and taking specialized classes at the trade school. So far, she's taken computer-aided design (CAD) classes and has added junior designer to her list of titles. Her next goal is to become a full-fledged die designer. Even though Dyke believes you can never know everything about this work, she certainly enjoys trying. The promotions and pay raises are just extra perks for all the learning.

REDEFINING HER JOB

The men still outnumber the women in machining, but Dyke has not let that slow her down. The work can be physically demanding, and her smaller size could be a drawback—if she let it. Instead, she's learned to rely on brains more than brawn to get the job done. Sometimes the stronger men will lift things not meant to be lifted in order to save time. Dyke doesn't even try it. She relies on her knowledge of physics and leaves the heavy work to hoists and pulleys. In the long run, it makes the job easier and safer—with a lot fewer backaches.

Manufacturing Engineer

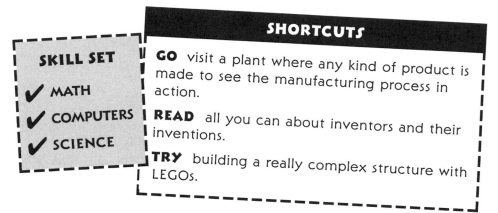

WHAT IS A MANUFACTURING ENGINEER?

A manufacturing engineer designs machines and processes that do things quicker and with greater ease than humans could do them. This practice is called automation, and it's the cornerstone of the manufacturing process. A manufacturing engineer starts with 200 basic manufacturing processes and more than 40,000 materials, and with these tools, he or she develops ways for making products that range in sophistication from chocolate chip cookies to jet fighters.

Sometimes manufacturing engineers develop processes to manufacture new products, and sometimes they develop new ways to manufacture already existing products. Other times manufacturing engineers devote their time to keeping manufacturing systems running smoothly, dealing with the vendors who provide the materials needed in manufacturing, and fine-tuning various manufacturing functions. Whether it's starting something new or maintaining an existing process, manufacturing engineers make sure their systems are safe, reliable, efficient, and productive. To do their jobs, manufacturing engineers rely on a combination of scientific and mathematical knowledge and experience, as well as good judgment and common sense.

Manufacturing engineers generally have at least a bachelor's degree in mechanical, electrical, or chemical engineering. This type of educational background, coupled with some experience, prepares them to take the lead in many types of manufacturing situations. Manufacturing engineers work in virtually any kind of industry that produces tangible products. Telecommunications, computer science, and other high-tech industries are currently hot areas of innovation in manufacturing; however, manufacturing engineers can be found in factories and plants that make anything from toilet paper or pencils to candy and soda.

Access to this profession can also be earned through a two-year degree in engineering technology. Engineering technicians get into the workplace and into the thick of things quicker, but the trade-off comes with fewer on-the-job responsibilities and lower pay. Technicians are part of a team under the guidance of full-fledged engineers and other types of professionals. It's an option to consider if you want to use your knowledge of math and science to solve real-life problems but don't want to pursue a four-year college degree just yet.

According to the American Society for Engineering Education (ASEE), there are a few questions you can ask yourself to find out if engineering might be a good career choice for you. These questions are

- Do you get good grades in math and science?
- Do you enjoy knowing how things work?
- Do you ever think of new or better ways to do things?
- If you get a gift that requires some assembly, do you put it together yourself?
- Do you like to work with computers and play video games?
- Do you like to do mazes and jigsaw puzzles?
- Do you usually make sound decisions, and do people trust your judgment?
- Can you express yourself easily and clearly?
- Do you work well with others?
- Do you like to know "why"?

If you answered yes to several of these questions, the ASEE says that your potential for success in engineering could be high. Of course, there's still plenty of time to work on communication skills, math and science grades, and the like. Start now to give yourself the best chance for success in this profession by taking as many math and science classes as you can. Work hard to get good grades, because that's the best way to get your foot in the door for an engineering career.

TRY IT OUT

VIRTUAL MANUFACTURING
All it takes is a computer linked to the Internet to get a look at several different kinds of manufacturing processes.

To see how cars are made, go to http://www.ipl.org/autou/aboutsite.html. Make sure to visit the Be a Champ, Play a Game section where you get a chance to design your very own manufacturing company.

Find out how those fields of cotton become your favorite T-shirt by touring the Russell Corporation's textile manufacturing plant at http://www.russellcorp.com/tour1.htm.

Discover how some of America's favorite candy is made in a specially guided tour of the M&M's factory by visiting http://www.m-ms.com/factory/tour.

Learn about the secret life of a Bic pen at http://www.bic-worldusa.com/coolstuff/how/index.htm.

For other virtual manufacturing tours, try some of the links listed at the student website of the Society of Manufacturing Engineers (http://www.manufacturingiscool.com) and click on the "tour where manufacturing happens" icon.

WHAT DID YOU DO ON YOUR SUMMER VACATION?

Thanks to the efforts of engineers and scientists everywhere, there are many summer camp programs all around the country where you can experience science and technology in ways very different from a regular classroom. These camps can be a great and fun link to learning now and earning a living down the road. For information about some scientific summer fun, visit the Society of Engineers' student website at http://www.manufacturingiscool.com and then click on the "making summer fun" icon, or look for opportunities that seem right for you from this book: *Summer Opportunities for Kids and Teenagers,* which is yearly updated by Peterson's Guides.

A SUGGESTED RESEARCH LIST

To find out if you have the right stuff to become an engineer, try some of the projects in the following books.

Goodwin, Robert H. *Engineering Projects for Young Scientists.* New York: Franklin Watts, 1987.

Salvadori, Mario G. *The Art of Construction: Projects and Principles for Beginning Engineers and Architects.* Chicago: Chicago Review Press, 1990.

Wood, Robert W. *Science for Kids: 39 Easy Engineering Experiments.* Blue Ridge Summit, Penn.: TAB Books, 1992.

For Internet links to all kinds of engineering activities, pay a visit to the Engineering: Your Future site at http://www.asee.org/precollege/html/fun_.htm.

Finally, for more information about engineering careers, try some of these titles.

Careers in Science and Engineering. Washington, D.C.: National Academy of Sciences, 1996.

Crabb, Howard. *The Virtual Engineer: 21st Century Product Development.* Washington, D.C.: Society of Manufacturing, 1998.

Garner, Geraldine O., and Kokrda Jacobs. *Careers in Engineering.* Lincolnwood, Ill.: VGM Career Horizons, 1993.

WHERE'S IT COME FROM?

Pick a product, any product, and trace its origins from beginning to end. For instance, say you choose a book like this one. You'd need to start the manufacturing process all the way back in the forest with the trees that were cut to make the paper. Then you'd move forward step by step.

Make a chart showing the entire process that you've chosen. Use library and Internet resources as well as your own common sense to figure out the manufacturing process.

JOIN THE CLUB

If you can find a teacher to sponsor the club and a few friends to join it, you have the makings of a Future Scientists and Engineers of America (FSEA) club. For more information write to FSEA, P.O. Box 9577, Anaheim, California 92812. For ideas for club projects visit the FSEA website at http://www2.fsea.org/FSEA.

CHECK IT OUT

American Society for Engineering Education
1818 N Street NW, Suite 600
Washington, D.C. 20036-2479
http://www.asee.org

Institute of Advanced Manufacturing Sciences
1111 Edison Drive
Cincinnati, Ohio 45216
http://www.iams.org

Junior Engineering Technical Society (JETS)
1420 King Street, Suite 405
Alexandria, Virginia 22314
http://www.jets.org

Society of Manufacturing Engineers
1 SME Drive
P.O. Box 930
Dearborn, Michigan 48121
http://www.sme.org

Society of Women Engineers
345 East 47th Street, Suite 305
New York, New York 10017
http://www.swe.org

Tooling and Manufacturing Association
1177 South Dee Road
Park Ridge, Illinois 60068
http://www.tmanet.com

GET ACQUAINTED

Jon Carver,
Manufacturing Engineer

CAREER PATH

CHILDHOOD ASPIRATION: To be an engineer.

FIRST JOB: Bag boy at a grocery store.

CURRENT JOB: Manager of equipment engineering for a major cosmetics manufacturing company.

Manufacturing Engineer

A PERFECT FIT
From the time Jon Carver was a boy, it was apparent that he was destined to become an engineer. He was always curious about what made things tick and was famous in his family for tearing things apart and trying to put them back together again. Every spare minute was spent building things with his Erector set.

When he got to high school, he ran track with a friend whose father owned a cosmetics plant. The friend helped him get a summer job working there, and Carver's education in manufacturing began with some firsthand experience.

AN INDIRECT PATH
In college. Carver decided to major in psychology instead of engineering after finding some of the engineering classes a bit boring for his taste. Although this is an unusual training choice for an engineer, Carver says that the most important thing an engineer needs to know is how to learn. He's found that as long as he knows where to find answers to problems and isn't afraid to ask technical experts for help, he's managed just fine.

LOOKING GOOD
Carver now works for a major cosmetics company that produces millions of units of more than 3,000 different products—everything from lipstick to shampoo. His job is to find equipment that automates the way these products are made and packaged as simply and inexpensively as possible.

This task often means integrating several different pieces of equipment into one production process. Once he's put together the best system he can find, he has to make sure that the equipment does what it's supposed to do and that all the equipment works well together for steps like filling, labeling, and capping. With some systems processing as many as 250 pieces a minute, you can understand how timing can be everything in this line of work.

A DAY IN THE LIFE OF A LIPSTICK

Carver and his colleagues go to an awful lot of trouble to make their customers look good. To get an idea of what's involved, consider what it takes to make a batch of lipstick.

First, the ingredients—waxes, pigments, and fragrance—are carefully mixed in huge vats. Then the vats are heated, and the mixture is blended.

Next, the lipstick mixture is poured into 5-gallon buckets and taken to the manufacturing plant where one of Carver's systems takes over. Here, the lipstick mixture is remelted and poured into molds. Once it solidifies, it's blown out into a lipstick tube.

Then it goes through a quality inspection to make sure it passes very stringent standards involving consistency and color, among other criteria. The lipsticks that pass the test move down an assembly line where machines put covers on each tube and apply labels. Farther down the line, the individual tubes of lipstick are sealed in plastic and packed into crates for shipment to customers.

ADVICE TO FUTURE MANUFACTURING ENGINEERS

According to Carver, the next generation of manufacturing engineers really have their work cut out for them. Their challenge will be to create high-tech automation systems that are as cost efficient as overseas labor. Right now, the trend is to have American goods produced in other countries where labor costs tend to be lower. It will take some exceptional engineering talent to stem that tide.

If you are up for that challenge, Carver says the best way you can prepare is to get a well-rounded education. Learn as much as you can about as much as you can. A broad, diverse background will open your mind to all the possibilities!

Market Researcher

SHORTCUTS

SKILL SET

✔ MATH

✔ WRITING

✔ TALKING

SHORTCUTS

GO take an informal survey of your class-mates or family members to find out the most popular television show on Tuesday nights.

READ the ads in a magazine and see if you can figure out the target market for each product.

TRY writing an ad to sell a favorite product to your friends.

WHAT IS A MARKET RESEARCHER?

A market researcher's job is to find out why people do the things they do and think the way they think. Whether it's finding out how people spend their weekends or what they think about political issues, a market researcher focuses on identifying various types of consumer wants and needs. He or she then uses this knowledge to assist businesses and other organizations in marketing their products, services, or ideas.

The American Marketing Association defines marketing as the process of planning and executing the conception, pricing, promotion, and distribution of ideas, good, and services to create exchanges that satisfy individual and organizational goals. Translated into simple terms, marketing means doing whatever it takes to get people to buy the products or services a company has to offer.

If that's what marketing is, then market research is the information-gathering process that links the person who needs or wants to buy something with the company that wants to sell it. This information can be used to identify the type of person most likely to buy a particular product (skateboard companies and senior citizens aren't a likely mix), to figure out the best ways to reach a target audience (via billboards, the Internet, television advertising, etc.), and to understand why (or why not) a particular kind of person would (or would not) buy certain goods.

Market research involves several steps, including

- identifying the product, service, or issue to be researched and learning all there is to know about it
- designing a way to collect the necessary information such as a telephone interview, a "stop the shoppers at the mall" survey, or a focus group
- managing the data collection process to make sure that scientific methods are used to get a fair and representative response
- compiling the results of the research using spreadsheets, special database programs, and other technological tools
- analyzing the results to determine their meaning
- explaining the findings and suggesting ways that clients can use the information to sell more products

For example, a market researcher hired by a shoe company that's getting ready to introduce a new line of sneakers for

teens might decide to go to malls in carefully selected parts of the country and interview a certain number of teens about their footwear preferences. The researcher might ask such questions as the following: Do you like these shoes? Would you wear shoes like these to school? How much would you be willing to pay for shoes like these? Where would you go to buy shoes like these?

The responses from all the teens would be compiled into a big report full of numbers, variables, and other types of statistical formulas. At this point, an experienced market researcher would look at the numbers to see if they indicate a successful product or a flop. Next, the researcher would write a report explaining the results and making recommendations about what the client should do with the sneakers. This part of the process involves equal parts of common sense, business savvy, and marketing know-how. The best researchers learn from experience and pay careful attention to successes and failures in the marketplace.

Some market researchers work exclusively for one company and are responsible only for that company's products. Other marketing researchers work for advertising agencies or market research firms and may conduct research on behalf of any number of clients. In either type of situation, a researcher's work can be summarized in these five tasks: designing research tools, collecting data, analyzing findings, reporting results, and making recommendations.

Market researchers must be comfortable with numbers on many levels. Statistics, spreadsheets, and data management are important tools used in this line of work. Skilled researchers know how to use computers to make these processes easier and more accurate. They also use computers to create reports and visually attractive presentations.

While some types of marketing positions do not require a college degree, people with hopes of advancing to positions of greater responsibility and higher earnings need a degree. This is certainly true for market researchers. A college degree in marketing, advertising, public relations, or another business-related major is essential.

Marketing is a very big industry that touches every product you could possibly think of. Some experts say that nearly 30 percent of the U.S. workforce is connected to marketing in some way. In addition to market research, there is a long list of related career options including advertising copywriter, lobbyist, public relations specialist, buyer, shopping mall manager, survey statistician, community service director, media marketing coordinator, press liaison, convention planner, literary agent, product manager, travel agent, publicist, account executive, recruiter, event coordinator, development officer, media buyer, media analyst, and product manager.

If this list seems wide and varied, that's because it is. A marketing background helps prepare you to write and speak well, to solve problems, to learn new information quickly, and to work well with others. These skills are in high demand and can lead to all kinds of opportunities for you.

TRY IT OUT

THE INSIDE SCOOP

You don't have to wait to find out what a market researcher does. All you need is a problem waiting to be solved, some carefully crafted questions, and a way to get answers from your fellow classmates.

Some issues you might want to tackle with your research include

- How do students like to spend their free time?
- What kinds of cafeteria foods do students like best?
- What kinds of after-school clubs and activities do students want to join?
- How can the rules at school be improved?
- Who gets the best grades in school—boys or girls?

Whatever the issue, come up with no less than 3 and no more than 10 questions to help clarify the issue. Be careful not to let your own prejudices get in the way of your questions. For instance, suppose you don't like the cafeteria food at your school. You want a better selection of lunchtime choices, and you think the perfect solution is to have your favorite pizzeria deliver every day. If you ask students what kind of pizza they want to have, you will color the results of the survey. For a more representative response, you might want to ask for suggestions about what foods other students would like to see on the menu.

Depending on which method you decide to use, you can either print copies of the survey and pass them out for people to fill out on their own, or you might arrange to sit in the cafeteria and personally interview several students. Once you tally up the results, write up a report and ask the principal to include the results in the school newspaper.

TARGET PRACTICE
One of the end results of market research is evident in the advertisements you see on billboards, in television commercials, and in various publications. Grab a stack of used newspapers and magazines and a pair of scissors. Go through the stack and cut out all the different ads you find.

Next, make little signs to designate three piles: one for children, one for teenagers, and one for adults. Look at each ad and identify which market the ad is trying to reach. Sort the adds into piles. Make notes about the types of words and other elements used to appeal to these different audiences.

A MARKETPLACE OF OPPORTUNITIES
The following books provide additional information about a variety of careers in marketing. Use them to figure out the best direction for your future career.

Camenson, Blythe, and Jan Goldberg. *Real People Working in Sales and Marketing.* Lincolnwood, Ill.: VGM Career Horizons, 1996.

Hird, Caroline, *Careers in Marketing, Advertising, and Public Relations.* London: Kogan Page, 1996.

Stair, Lila, and Sarah Kennedy. *Careers in Marketing.* Lincolnwood, Ill.: VGM Career Horizons, 1995.

Steinberg, Margery. *Opportunities in Marketing Careers.* Lincolnwood, Ill.: VGM Career Horizons, 1993.

CYBERSHOPPING

When it comes to marketing, the Internet is quickly becoming an effective sales tool for all kinds of companies. Check out some of the companies shopping for your business on the Internet. Pick a favorite product or television show and use an Internet search engine such as Hotbot (http://www.hotbot.com) or Yahoo! (http://www.yahoo.com) to find its website. Also try some of these company websites.

- McDonald's   http://www.mcdonalds.com
- Frito-Lay   http://www.fritolay.com
- PepsiCo   http://www.pepsiworld.com
- Nike   http://www.nike.com
- Adidas   http://www.adidas.com
- Nickelodeon   http://www.nick.com
- Disney Company   http://disney.go.com

Make a chart to compare how effective each site is in grabbing your attention and getting you involved in their pitch.

CHECK IT OUT

American Advertising Federation
1101 Vermont Avenue NW, Suite 500
Washington, D.C. 20005-6306
http://www.aaf.org

American Marketing Association
250 South Wacker Drive, Suite 200
Chicago, Illinois 60606
http://www.ama.org

Marketing Research Association
1344 Silas Deane Highway, Suite 306
Rocky Hill, Connecticut 06067-0230
http://www.mra-net.com

Public Relations Society of America
33 Irving Place
New York, New York 10003-2376
http://www.prsa.org

Women in Advertising and Marketing
4200 Wisconsin Avenue, Suite 106-238
Washington, D.C. 20016

GET ACQUAINTED

Amy Steiner Schafrann,
Market Researcher

CAREER PATH

CHILDHOOD ASPIRATION: To be a dancer at first and a psychologist as she got older.

FIRST JOB: Counselor at a summer day camp.

CURRENT JOB: Managing partner at Yankelovich Partners, one of the country's leading market research and consulting firms.

LESSON LEARNED

Amy Steiner Schafrann went to college to pursue a degree in psychology. She got sidetracked after taking a marketing methods course. During the semester, her marketing professor asked her to be his research assistant, and she discovered through work and class that she really liked it. This experience introduced a whole new way to blend her interest in psychology with a career in marketing.

A MARKETING MARVEL

Schafrann began her marketing career by working at an international research company. She worked there for three years and then moved to a big New York advertising agency. There she continued to move up through the ranks and was eventually promoted to senior vice president of market research and planning. It was an important job and one that did not go unnoticed.

Her work there was so exceptional that she was selected by *Advertising Age*, a prestigious magazine in the field, as one of the 100 Best and Brightest Young People in Advertising. She was also elected to the YMCA's Academy of Women Achievers. Both of these honors recognize the commitment and creativity Schafrann consistently applies to her work.

Schafrann has been with her current company, Yankelovich Partners, for more than 10 years. According to her official résumé, her responsibilities include managing both custom and syndicated products, marketing strategy development and targeting, segmentation, communications testing, new concept and product testing, and customer satisfaction. It makes for an interesting and very busy work life.

LEADING THE WAY

Now that Schafrann has become one of the "bosses" in her company, she's found that a key to her success is hiring good people, showing them the ropes, and watching them succeed. She's learned to give people credit where it's due and to compensate them fairly for their efforts.

STORYTELLING WITH NUMBERS

Schafrann says she has always liked math and often prefers to add numbers in her head than use a calculator. It's a good thing that she's so comfortable with numbers, because she sees plenty of them in her line of work. In fact, one of Schafrann's favorite parts of her job is taking numerical results of a research study and finding the story that they tell. A big part of her job is to make the numbers come alive and to capture the truths they represent about each client's project. It's a process that Schafrann has learned to do well.

KID STUFF

One of the big projects that Schafrann manages is called the Yankelovich/Nickelodeon Youth Monitor. For more than a decade now, this project has studied 6- to 16-year-old kids from all over the country to find out what they are doing, what their worries are, what their dreams are, and what they hope for the future. Nickelodeon, the project's joint sponsor, uses the information to make programming decisions for their cable television channel, to design new shows for this market, and to develop programs that involve kids in their communities.

You can take a peek at Schafrann's work at the Yankelovich website (http://www.yankelovich.com).

Mathematician

SHORTCUTS

SKILL SET

✔ MATH
✔ COMPUTERS
✔ SCIENCE

GO piece together a 3-D puzzle and put your math logic skills to work.

READ *Mathematics from the Birth of Numbers* by Jan Gullberg and Peter Hilton (New York: W.W. Norton, 1997) for an interesting introduction to the world of numbers.

TRY making a list of all the ways math is used in everyday life. Put some thought into it and you'll come up with a very long list!

WHAT IS A MATHEMATICIAN?

Here's a career that really adds up. Mathematician is consistently ranked by *Jobs Rated Almanac* as one of the top five careers (on the basis of salary, benefits, outlook for the future, stress level, work environment, and job security). It is a career that offers a surprising number of options and provides challenge, discovery, and a chance to make a real difference in the world.

Simply put, mathematicians are problem solvers. They use mathematical theories and techniques along with the latest technology to solve all kinds of economic, scientific, engineering, and business problems. A mathematician might use various mathematical modeling and computational methods to figure out, for instance, the best way for an airline to schedule flights to 150 locations using 64 jets. Or they might determine the effectiveness of a new drug by analyzing data on several thousand test patients.

Some mathematicians, called **theoretical mathematicians,** enjoy discovering new mathematical rules and finding new ways to use math ideas. They are in constant pursuit of answers to their questions about why things work the way they do. They look for patterns in the world around them and get great satisfaction in giving logical proofs (evidence) to their claims.

Theoretical mathematicians often teach in colleges or universities, and many now work in industrial research labs. Their new discoveries helps further important advances in science, technology, and engineering.

Other mathematics, called **applied mathematicians,** use mathematics in practical ways to do their job. That means that they apply mathematical principles to real-life problems. Recent work has involved developing ways for people to buy products over the Internet, called electronic commerce, and achieving major advances in the ways people communicate with each other through technology such as pagers and cellular phones. In addition, some mathematicians are helping biologists understand the mathematical codes found in human genes and are doing important work to crack DNA (deoxyribonucleic) codes. The applied side of mathematics can be particularly exciting because mathematicians can actually see the results of their work in new technology and new systems.

Mathematicians work in all kinds of places including business, industry, government, and education. You'll find plenty of mathematicians in the computer and the communications industries, as well as in oil companies, banks, insurance companies, security and commodity exchanges, pharmaceutical com-

panies, and consulting firms. Mathematicians also work for almost every branch of the federal government. Sometimes they are assigned to top-secret projects for agencies such as the Department of Defense or the National Security Agency.

Probably the single most common characteristic of a successful mathematician is curiosity. Once intrigued with a problem, a mathematician seeks to solve it with a combination of logic, intuition, and imagination, often experiencing countless rounds of bad guesses before finding the final solution.

As you might have guessed by now, becoming a mathematician requires a good education with a strong background in math. A bachelor's degree in mathematics is a must, and for many positions, it is only the starting point. You can start preparing yourself now by taking courses in algebra, geometry, and calculus. Taking these classes helps build your brain power and gets you thinking like a mathematician.

TRY IT OUT

MAGICAL MATH

Who says math can't be fun? Try some of the activities in the following books and amaze your family and friends with your mathematical magic.

Blum, Ray. *Math Tricks, Puzzles and Games.* New York: Sterling, 1995.

Julius, Edward H. *Arithmetricks: 50 Easy Ways to Add, Subtract, Multiply and Divide Without a Calculator.* New York: John Wiley and Sons, 1995.

Maganzini, Christy. *Cool Math: Math Tricks, Amazing Math Activities, Cool Calculations, Awesome Math Factoids and More.* Los Angeles: Price Stern Sloan Publishing, 1998.

You can also try a little sleuthing around with some math mysteries in William Johnson's *25 Mini Math Mysteries* (New York: Scholastic, 1998).

Other highly regarded math resources you are sure to enjoy include

————————————

Burns, Marilyn. *The Book of Think: Or How, to Solve a Problem Twice Your Size.* New York: Little, Brown, 1976.
———. *The I Hate Mathematics! Book.* New York: Little, Brown, 1976.
———. *Math for Smarty Pants.* New York: Little, Brown, 1982.

————————————

WHY STUDY MATH?

You're sitting in pre-algebra class, and your teacher is going on and on about multiple exponents. The only brain cell currently awake in your body suddenly screams, "why do I need to know this stuff anyway?" If you've ever experienced a similar reaction to a seemingly endless math lecture, you'll want to check out some answers given by many interesting math professionals at the website of the Mathematical Association of America (http://www.maa.org/careers/index.html).

GIRLS COUNT TOO

Math is one of those professions that has tended to attract more males than females in years past. Fortunately, recent studies have shown that there is no reason why women can't achieve the same level of success in this area as men. So, girls, get out there and start counting the career opportunities in one of the fastest growing professional fields! And, boys, don't worry. There's plenty of opportunity for all of you.

For a historical overview of women's role in mathematics, read *Women in Mathematics* by Lynn M. Osen (Cambridge, Mass.: MIT Press, 1975). For a more contemporary look at what 38 women are achieving in this field, as well as challenging real-life math problems to solve, check out *She Does Math! Real Life Problems from Women on the Job,* edited by Marla Parker (Washington, D.C.: Mathematical Association of America, 1995). Finally, for in-depth stories about successful women mathematicians, plus some challenging math activities, you'll want to read Teri Perl's *Women and Numbers: Lives of Women Mathematicians* (San Carlos, Calif.: Wide World Publishing, 1997).

IT ALL ADDS UP

Go on-line to the Math Forum and join students and teachers from around the world in solving math-related "problems of the week." There are creative challenges for both the elementary and middle school students in geometry, algebra, trigonometry, and calculus. See how far you can go at http://forum.swarthmore.edu.

THE DOCTOR IS IN

Have a question about math? Ask Dr. Math. This on line resource includes an amazing array of math resources from the elementary level all the way through high school and beyond. Browse through an assortment of mathematical topics and see if you can stump the experts by submitting your own questions to http://forum.swarthmore.edu//dr.math.

MORE MATH FUN AND GAMES

One more website you'll want to visit is Mathmania (http://csr.uvic.ca/~mmania). Here you'll find a challenging variety of puzzles, stories, activities, and other interesting math resources. For example, you can make the connection between math and roller coasters, untie the mathematical mysteries of knots, and see how something as dull sounding as graph theory becomes fun when you know how to use it.

CHECK IT OUT

American Mathematical Society
P.O. Box 6248
Providence, Rhode Island 02940-6248
http://www.ams.org

Association for Women in Mathematics
4114 Computer and Space Sciences Building
University of Maryland
College Park, Maryland 20742-2461
http://www.awm-math.org

Mathematical Association of America
1529 18th Street NW
Washington, D.C. 20036-1385
800-741-9415
http://www.maa.org

National Council of Teachers of Mathematics
1906 Association Drive
Reston, Virginia 22091-1593
http://www.nctm.org

Society for Industrial and Applied Mathematics
3600 University City Science Center
Philadelphia, Pennsylvania 19104-2688
http://www.siam.org.

GET ACQUAINTED

Lenore Blum, Mathematician

CAREER PATH

CHILDHOOD ASPIRATION: To be a mathematician.

FIRST JOB: Summer camp counselor.

CURRENT JOB: Distinguished career professor at Carnegie Mellon University where one of her highest priorities is to develop a model program for women in computer science.

A SMART COOKIE

Lenore Blum was born in New York City but moved with her family to Caracas, Venezuela, when she was still a young girl. This international experience provided some interesting educational and cultural experiences for Blum. It was in Caracas that she first discovered math as a fascinating, exciting subject waiting to be explored. Her love affair with math began with long division. She caught on to this concept instantly and kept learning all she could. Before long, she became known as the school's best student in math and graduated from high school when she was just 16.

When it came time to go to college, she initially followed a teacher's bad advice. She had wanted to major in mathematics, but the teacher told her that it was a "dead" field and that everything important had been discovered 2,000 years ago. Blum assumed that the only option was to blend mathematics with another subject in order to make it work, so Blum, also artistic and creative, decided to combine mathematics and art and pursue a degree in architecture.

By the second year of college, however, Blum was certain that mathematics was the way she wanted to go with her studies. Nothing challenged her as much or gave her as much satisfaction as figuring out complex mathematical formulas and truly understanding how all the pieces in the process fit together. She switched majors during her second year of college and has never regretted the decision.

DOING THE IMPOSSIBLE

Blum pursued her dream of becoming a mathematician at a time when women mathematicians were very rare. In fact, one of life's early disappointments came for Blum on the day she learned that she would not be admitted to the Massachusetts Institute of Technology (MIT), one of the best schools in mathematical sciences, to begin her college studies. It wasn't that she wasn't smart enough; the problem was her gender. Blum was a woman, and as one admissions officer told her, "MIT is no place for women." Princeton University, another prestigious school, did not even admit women until 1968—the same year that Blum earned her Ph.D.

The fact that Blum accomplished something that others thought couldn't or shouldn't be done says a great deal about her commitment to the profession. She had to overcome many obstacles to reach her professional goals and, in doing so, opened doors to greater opportunities for women in mathematics.

After distinguishing herself by hard work and dedication, Blum was eventually admitted to MIT to complete her graduate work. As it turned out, MIT *was* a place for this woman after all.

A CAREER THAT COUNTS

Blum's career officially began as a lecturer at the University of Berkeley in one of the best mathematics departments in the country. She worked there for two years and then was told she wouldn't be rehired. This was during the late 1960s when high-level opportunities for women in math were few and far between.

Blum realized that this situation would not change unless someone did something, so she joined a group of colleagues in forming the Association for Women in Mathematics. It didn't take long for her to build a reputation as an expert on women and mathematics.

Later she was hired to teach an algebra class at Mills College, an all-women's school. The course she was supposed to teach was so dull that she carefully designed a new one that introduced math as a link to new opportunities for young women. Her success in this effort led to a promotion as the head of a brand-new math and computer science department at the college.

BACK TO THE DRAWING BOARD

Eventually, Blum decided to devote all her professional energies to mathematical research. Her early work as a researcher focused on model theory, and she is credited with formulating new methods of logic to solve old problems in algebra. She has also worked with her husband, Manuel, to design computers that can learn the same way that small children do—by examples.

You can get an idea of how complex Blum's work is just by reading the titles of some of her published work: *On a Theory of Computation Over the Real Numbers: NP Completeness,*

Recursive Functions and Universal Machines; Towards an Asymptotic Analysis of Karmarkar's Algorithm; and *Complexity and Real Computation.* Don't let these technical titles scare you away from mathematics. Blum says this type of work is what she presents to fellow mathematicians. She also puts a lot of effort into making sure that everyday people can understand (and get excited about) mathematics.

A WORLD OF MATH

Blum's work has left its mark in places all over the world. She has made presentations at conferences throughout the United States and in Europe, China, Japan, Southeast Asia, the former Soviet Union, Latin America, and Africa. At the 1991 Pan-American Congress of Mathematicians, Blum represented the American Mathematical Society. The conference was held in Nairobi, Kenya, that year and made such an impression on Blum that she was inspired to start building links between the North American and African mathematics communities. Since then she has worked hard to construct an electronic communications link between the two continents.

According to Blum, jet-setting around the world is one of the hidden benefits of becoming a mathematician. With math, there are no borders between countries, and everyone speaks almost the same language. She sees the chance that math provides for people of different nationalities to work together on common problems as an important key to world peace.

A CHAMPION FOR THE CAUSE

Blum is especially well known for her efforts to get more girls involved in math. Aside from being a founding member of the Association for Women in Mathematics, she served as its president for several years. In addition, she helped create the Math/Science Network, which sponsors Expanding Your Horizons conferences around the country to get girls interested in math and science. Blum is credited for encouraging many young women to consider careers in math-intensive fields.

Throughout her career, Blum has served as a worthy role model for women in math. She's even earned such distinctions as becoming the first female editor of the prestigious *International Journal of Algebra and Computation* and being elected vice president of the American Mathematical Society. Suffice it to say that the success she's enjoyed during her career is worthy of emulation by mathematical minds of both genders.

You can read more about Blum's career in *Women and Numbers: Lives of Women Mathematicians* by Teri Perl (San Carlos, Calif.: Wide World Publishing, 1997).

Purchasing Agent

SKILL SET

✔ BUSINESS

✔ MATH

✔ TALKING

WHAT IS A PURCHASING AGENT?

Do you like shopping? Are you a bargain hunter? Does the idea of spending millions of dollars of someone else's money sound exciting? If so, you might want to think about becoming a purchasing agent. A purchasing agent buys the goods, materials, and services that a business needs to do business.

Any company that buys at least $100,000 worth of materials needs a purchasing agent, or buyer. The military, all levels of government, restaurant chains, department stores, and hospitals are just a few of the places where you will find a purchasing agent employed. In addition, all types of retail stores use buyers. Whether it's a sporting goods store or a jewelry store, someone has to decide what products the store's customers are most likely to buy and make sure that ample supplies are available at the appropriate time.

Buying for a major corporation isn't exactly like going on a gigantic spending spree with thousands and sometimes even millions of dollars to spend. The buying decisions made by purchasing agents must be based on the best information avail-

able. That means that purchasing agents have to shop around to find the best materials or services, the best price, and the most reliable delivery. To achieve this, purchasing agents may review listings in catalogs, industry periodicals, and trade journals, attend trade shows and visit suppliers' worksites. In addition, they must research the track records of various suppliers, and they must advertise to let suppliers know of their company's needs.

Remember, profits are the name of the game for any viable business. Successful buyers guard the bottom line and diligently seek out the best materials for the best price. They must also make sure that they get the right amounts at the right time, which takes enormous amounts of managerial skill and market awareness. All in all, purchasing agents must do a lot of careful planning, have a good understanding of their own business and its customers, and put strong negotiating skills to use on a regular basis.

To do their job, purchasing agents generally come to rely on a wide variety of vendors—companies who sell the goods they need. By carefully nurturing good business relationships and building a team of suppliers, purchasing agents are assured of good service and quality products. Computer technology also comes in extremely handy to help purchasing agents keep track of all the details and budget considerations.

In smaller companies, purchasing agents might be responsible for buying all the materials that a company uses, including everything from toilet paper to computer systems. In larger companies, purchasing agents are often more specialized. They may be responsible for purchasing the materials for a specific product or for a specific department. For instance, a buyer in a snack food company might be responsible for buying potatoes for potato chips, while a purchaser in a department store might be responsible for buying all the clothes sold in the children's department.

Most purchasing agents, especially those who work for larger companies or for the government, have college degrees in business, purchasing or supply management, or another related field. Two professional organizations offer certification programs for purchasers. The American Purchasing Society offers the certified purchasing professional (CPP) credential to those who meet certain requirements of integrity, education, and experience. The National Association of Purchasing Managers offers two levels of certification: the accredited purchasing practitioner (APP) and the certified purchasing manager (CPM) certifications. Both require that applicants pass an exam and meet specific education and experience criteria.

Other career options that are similar in scope to purchasing include industrial distribution, logistics and transportation management, and operations management.

TRY IT OUT

PARTY TIME!

The best homework assignment for a future purchasing agent is this: Throw a party! It's a fun way to find out if you've got the "super shopper" skills you'll need to succeed in this career. Here's what you'll need to do.

First, make your plans. Set a budget and make your guest list. Decide what supplies you'll need to have a good time: food, decorations, prizes, etc. Make a list of everything you'll need. Leave room on the list to write down information about prices and suppliers.

Next, start shopping around. Find out who sells what you need and how much it costs. Write the prices and suppliers on your list. The shopping inserts in the Sunday newspaper are a good source of information. You'll also want to tag along with your parents when they go shopping. Don't forget to take your list.

Third, make your decisions. Look at your list and compare products and prices. Who offers the best products for the lowest price? You may find that you'll need to buy from more than one store to get the best bargains. Total up the costs of each of your items. Does it fit within your budget?

Fourth, figure out how to get the products from the stores to the party location. Maybe some of the stores provide delivery service. If not, you'll have to make a plan for picking them up yourself. Think of the most efficient way to make all the required stops in one trip.

And finally, put everything together, put on some music, and let the party begin!

After all the guests go home, take stock of how it went. Was there enough food and other supplies to satisfy all your guests? Are there too many leftovers? Did you stay within your budget? Did everyone have a good time? If you got the right answers, congratulate yourself for a purchasing job well done.

OPEN FOR BUSINESS

Pick any type of store that you would like to own. Now, imagine what kinds of products you'd want to sell at your store.

Keep thinking while you gather a notebook, scissors, glue, and plenty of newspapers and magazines. Start the purchasing process by finding pictures of products you'd want to sell. Clip the pictures, glue them to a page in your notebook, and make notes about available color, sizes, and prices. See if you can find sources that offer better prices or selection and start a new page for them.

After you've exhausted your supply of publications, go online and do some cyber shopping. Try to find an interesting selection of products at good prices. Of course, if this were a real store you were starting, you'd want to secure wholesale prices that are at least half of the retail price you'd pay at a store. But this exercise will give you an idea of what the purchasing process is like and the types of tools (written and electronic) that a purchaser might use to do his or her job.

If you have access to America Online, just click into the AOL Shopping Channel and pick the category that best fits your store. Here you'll find everything from apparel and automobiles to pets and toys. An alternative to America Online is to use your favorite search engine either to run a general "shopping" search or to look for one of your favorite product lines, such as Gap at http://www.gap.com or Nike at http://www.nike.com.

A MILLION IDEAS

What if you had $1 million to spend? How much could you buy? How far would it go?

It's not at all unusual for purchasing agents to work with that much money and more in a given year's budget. To get an idea of what it would be like, get a big sheet of poster board. In the middle, use a marker to write $1,000,000. Now find pictures and prices of all the things you could buy if you had that much money. Be generous and have fun. Don't stop this fantasy spending spree until the money is all gone.

CHECK IT OUT

American Purchasing Society
11910 Oak Trail Way
Port Richey, Florida 34668
http://www.american-purchasing.com/index2.htm

National Association of Purchasing Management
P.O. Box 22160
Tempe, Arizona 85282
http://www.napm.org

National Contract Management Association
1912 Woodford Road
Vienna, Virginia 22182
800-344-8096

National Institute of Governmental Purchasing
151 Spring Street, Suite 300
Hendron, Virginia 20170-5223
http://www.nigp.org

National Retail Federation
100 West 31st Street
New York, New York 10001

GET ACQUAINTED

Craig Leafgren,
Purchasing Agent

CAREER PATH

CHILDHOOD ASPIRATION: To be a farmer.

FIRST JOB: Researcher working to develop better potatoes for a major snack food manufacturer.

CURRENT JOB: Manager of merchandising equipment procurement for an international snack food company.

A FARM BOY

Craig Leafgren grew up on a farm where growing potatoes, onions, and other vegetables was a way of life. He was active in 4-H clubs while young and won several prizes in 4-H competitions for calves and horses he raised. Leafgren loved working with the crops and the animals, so when it came time for college, a degree in agronomy was a natural choice.

THE FRESH CHIP GAME

At a major snack food company Leafgren's work group is responsible for buying the wire and corrugated materials that his company's snack food products are displayed on in stores. Before he reached this management position, he was responsible for a variety of other purchasing activities involving potatoes, corn, vegetable oil, and packaging.

In order to purchase the right quantities of materials to display millions of packages of snack foods, Leafgren has to answer questions such as

- How much of this product will customers want to buy at different times of the year?
- If the product is put on sale for a lower price, how much more will the customer buy?
- What kind of package will attract customers' attention and make them want to buy the product?
- What kind of information must be included on the package, including the nutritional facts required by the government?
- How many packages can be produced at the supplier each day?

The answers to those questions determine how much Leafgren buys, what he buys, and where he sends all the materials.

NEVER A DULL MOMENT

Leafgren's work has never been boring. He likes working with fun food products and enjoys the challenge of doing his best work. Leafgren has also discovered that working with a large corporation offers plenty of opportunity to learn new skills and advance to higher levels of responsibility.

Leafgren's favorite project was big, fast, and complicated. It involved "rolling out" a new snack chip in new packaging for a special national promotion. The best part of the project was that it worked. People bought the product like crazy. After working so hard to get the product ready to sell, Leafgren enjoyed watching it become such a big success.

HAVING A BAD CHIP DAY

Anytime you are working with so much product and so many vendors, there is always room for problems. However, at an international company, there's usually no such thing as a "little" glitch.

Take, for example, the time a vendor printed the wrong bar code on a 4th of July shipment of chips. The bar code is that series of black lines on the back of a product that merchants use to scan the price and product information into their computerized cash registers. It doesn't sound like such a big deal to mess up a little black line or two. But, when you are talking about several truckloads of product going out to merchants all over the country, those misplaced black lines quickly become a very big deal—and a very big headache for purchasing agents.

TIPS FOR FUTURE PURCHASERS

Leafgren advises not to worry if you don't know exactly what career you want to pursue. Get a good education and find an industry that you like. Leafgren says that there are lots of different ways to become a purchasing agent. In fact, while one of Leafgren's bosses used to be a school teacher, Leafgren started out as an agronomist specializing in potatoes, and other coworkers began as engineers or marketing specialists. What they all have in common is the ability to work hard, learn fast, and make good decisions.

Stockbroker

WHAT IS A STOCKBROKER?

A stockbroker's job is to invest other people's money in the stock market. Whether it's an investment of a few hundred dollars or a few million, a stockbroker works with individual clients to develop an "investment portfolio" that best meets their financial goals. For instance, some people prefer investments that have the potential to earn a big return in a short amount of time. These risk-takers have to be carefully positioned to enjoy the gains yet sustain the inevitable losses that come with this type of investing. Other clients may prefer safe, steady investments that provide a profit over time.

To satisfy the needs of all kinds of clients, a stockbroker must know how the stock market works, must be extremely knowledgeable about all kinds of investments, and must stay current on the constantly changing financial status of a wide variety of investment options. In addition, a stockbroker must be able to convey all this information to clients in a way that wins their trust—and their investment capital.

Some stockbrokers work in an office managing their clients' investments, and some actually trade on the floor of the stock market. Either way, a stockbroker's work is fast paced and intense. Stockbrokers often have to think fast, using both well-researched information and their own good instincts.

Stockbrokers spend a lot of time on the telephone and may talk with 50 to 100 clients each day. They also read what one stockbroker estimated to be about "10 pounds" of financial information daily. The only effective stockbroker is an informed

stockbroker. Yesterday's news is often not good enough in a profession where fortunes can be made and lost overnight.

Stockbrokers can work anywhere—in big cities and little towns. When they want to buy or sell stock for one of their customers, they have to place an order with a floor trader who works in a stock exchange. The New York Stock Exchange is the oldest and biggest exchange. There are also exchanges in San Francisco, Chicago, Boston, Cincinnati, and Philadelphia, as well as in different parts of the world.

In some ways, U.S. stock exchanges are much like they were a century ago. Traders still congregate in pits and make trades by yelling out offers. Deals worth millions of dollars are made by one trader negotiating a price with another trader. Their word is all it takes to close the sale.

In other ways, stock exchanges are a great example of the wonders of modern technology. Thousands of miles of communication lines link stockbrokers in offices all over the country to traders in exchanges worldwide. This high-tech arrangement allows a stockbroker in London to order stock from a floor trader in Los Angeles in a matter of minutes. In addition, cellular phones and pagers have added to the breakneck speed and the efficiency of floor trading.

In order to trade on the floor of a stock exchange, floor traders must either belong to a firm that has a "seat" on the exchange or purchase one for themselves for $600,000. Of course, having a seat on the exchange is a bit misleading. Floor traders are generally on their feet all day, rushing from pit to pit making bids.

Becoming a stockbroker does not require a college degree, although most stockbrokers have one. It does require passing the General Securities Registered Representative Examination, which a person can take after being employed by a brokerage firm for at least four months. In some states stockbrokers also have to pass the Uniform Securities Agents State Law Examination. This process is meant to be a safeguard to ensure that stockbrokers know what they are doing before they start dealing with other people's money.

TRY IT OUT

PLAY THE STOCK MARKET GAME

The Stock Market Game is a computer-based simulation that helps kids understand how the stock market works. The game allows teams of students to invest an imaginary $100,000 in the stock market.

The Stock Market Game is used in school districts all over the country. If your school doesn't have access to it, request information about acquiring it from the Securities Industry Association, 120 Broadway, 35th Floor, New York, New York 10271-0090, or check out the game's website at http://www.smg2000.org.

BULL OR BEAR MARKET?

Another way to learn about the stock market and see how it can work for you is to tap into the resources at a website called Edustock at http://library.advanced.org/3088. Along with helpful tutorials, the site includes easy-to-read company profiles on well-known companies such as Coca-Cola and

McDonald's. Once you've got a little knowledge tucked away, click into the stock market simulation, pick up $100,000 in virtual cash, and start trading with real-time accurate stock data (20-minute delay). The site offers a great way to learn about the stock market without risking your life savings.

READ YOUR WAY INTO THE INSIDE TRACK

For a good, basic introduction to how the stock market works, consult Nancy Dunnan's book entitled *The Stock Market* (New York: Silver Burdett Press, 1990). Two books by Jack D. Schwager will give you the secrets of some of the top traders of Wall Street: *Market Wizards: Interviews with Top Traders* (New York: HarperBusiness, 1993) and *The New Market Wizards: Conversations with America's Top Traders* (New York: HarperBusiness, 1994). And for all the gory details about the worst stock market crash in history, read either *Black Tuesday: The Stock Market Crash of 1929* (Brookfield, Conn.: Millbrook Press, 1995) by Barbara Silberdick Feinberg or *The Stock Market Crash of 1929.* (Parsippany, N.J.: Silver Burdett Press, 1994) by Nancy Millichap Davies.

GO FOR THE GUSTO!

For those who can't decide which they like best—playing sports or making money—here's your chance to have it all. Use your computer to access SportShares website (http://www.sportshares.com). This free Internet game combines the excitement of fantasy sports with the challenge of the stock market by converting teams and players from the professional sports world into stocks that you buy and sell.

Your goal is to build and manage an account of fantasy shares that outperforms the competition in an effort to win fame and fortune. There are links to all your favorite professional sports teams, and you can take your pick of which game to play: fantasy baseball, basketball, football, golf, hockey, NASCAR, or soccer.

CHECK IT OUT

American Financial Services Association
919 18th Street NW
Washington, D.C. 20006

American Stock Exchange
86 Trinity Place
New York, New York 10006
800-THE-AMEX
http://www.amex.com

Association for Investment Management and Research
P.O. Box 3668
Charlottesville, Virginia
22903

Chicago Board of Options Exchange
LaSalle at Van Buren
Chicago, Illinois 60605
800-OPTIONS
http://www.cboe.com

New York Stock Exchange
11 Wall Street
New York, New York 10005
800-692-6973
http://www.nyse.com

Pacific Stock Exchange
301 Pine Street
San Francisco, California 94104
800-TALK-PSE

Philadelphia Stock Exchange
1900 Market Street
Philadelphia, Pennsylvania 19103
800-THE-PHLX
http://www.phlx.com

Securities Industry Association
120 Broadway
New York, New York 10271
http://www.sia.com

GET ACQUAINTED

Ron Bruder,
Options Market Maker/Trader

CAREER PATH

CHILDHOOD ASPIRATION: To help other people.

FIRST JOB: Recreational therapist for the deaf and blind.

CURRENT JOB: Designated primary market maker working on the Chicago Board of Options Exchange.

CREAM OF THE CROP

Ron Bruder is one of 23 designated primary market makers (DPMs) who trade stock options at the Chicago Board Options Exchange. With more than 1,000 regular traders on the floor, it is easy to recognize that DPMs are a special kind of trader. DPMs are selected by the board to represent some of the best stock options on the market. DPMs have a good reputation for keeping the rules of the exchange and must demonstrate a high degree of integrity.

A CHANGE OF PLANS

Bruder actually started his career in an educational field. After graduating from college, he worked with deaf and blind people as a recreational therapist. He found this work very satisfying and a natural extension of all the volunteer work he'd done in junior high and high school.

He had always been fascinated with the stock market however, so when a college contact offered him an opportunity to work as retail stockbroker at a firm in Arizona, he decided to give it a try. Training to be a floor trader in Chicago was an on-the-job, learn-as-you-go process that required reading lots of books, mostly mathematical ones.

A TYPICAL DAY ON THE JOB

With the excitement of following the ups and downs of the stock market, no two days are ever exactly alike, but the following sketch will give you an idea of the way Bruder's days tend to look.

4:30 A.M. Bruder is up and at 'em printing out a 100-page report on his computer that recaps the previous day's activity. It also tells him if it was a profitable day or not.

5:30 A.M. Bruder leaves for the office with cell phone and financial papers in tow.

6:30 A.M. Bruder meets with other staff members to assign tasks and talk about the strategy for the day.

7:30 A.M. Bruder takes advantage of the quiet time before the market opens to do paperwork and read financial newspapers such as the *Wall Street Journal* and *Investor's Business Daily*.

8:30 A.M. Market opens and Bruder starts his daily trading marathon. Every once in a while he sneaks in time for a quick lunch or snack.

3:10 P.M. Market closes and Bruder clears up paperwork, shuts down the trading floor computers, and goes upstairs to his office.

3:15 P.M. Bruder finds just enough time to squeeze in a staff meeting and an occasional training session for new brokers.

4:30 P.M. Time to head for home unless one of the exchange committees that Bruder serves on has a scheduled meeting.

WEATHERING THE UPS AND DOWNS

Bruder says that you must have nerves of steel to work in the trading pit all day. Knowing how much money is riding on your every move can be a little scary. He says that the best days are those in which he's gained several hundred thousand dollars for his clients. The worst days are just the opposite!

ADVICE FOR FUTURE STOCKBROKERS

Bruder has two tips for aspiring stockbrokers: Learn how to get along with all kinds of people and learn how to think and work quickly and accurately. He also notes that one of the most basic skills for a stockbroker or floor trader is the ability to add and subtract large numbers in their head. Brokers work with millions of dollars every day, so accuracy is everything.

ALMOST AS GOOD AS BEING THERE

While nothing is quite as exciting as actually experiencing a day at the Chicago stock exchange where Bruder works, you can enjoy a look at a pictorial history of the exchange from 1928 to present at http://www.chicagostockex.com/photo/ph1_5.html.

Traffic Planner

SKILL SET

✔ MATH

✔ COMPUTERS

✔ WRITING

WHAT IS A TRAFFIC PLANNER?

Red light. Green light. Rush-hour traffic. Car pool lanes. Subway lines. If you are like most people, you seldom ever think about why they work the way they do. But no matter where you go, someone has spent countless hours figuring out the safest and most efficient way to get you there. Traffic planners are those "someones." A traffic planner's work is devoted to designing safe and efficient transportation systems.

This work might be as complex as planning a new six-lane urban highway system or as challenging as solving parking problems. A traffic planner might design a public transit system for a sprawling metropolitan area or research the best way to divert traffic through a busy business district. The main function of some traffic planners is to plan the timing of traffic lights.

Traffic planners also keep track of how many vehicles typically use specific roads. They use special equipment, such as underground pneumatic tubes, radar, or photoelectric detectors, to conduct traffic counts. They also keep track of traffic accidents to determine if action can be taken to prevent future ones.

City and state governments are one of the main employers of traffic planners in their highway or streets departments. Other employers include federal highway agencies, county highway departments, private consulting firms, colleges and universities, and some types of businesses.

A career choice that is closely linked to traffic planner is transportation engineer. Transportation engineers design highways, airports, and public transit systems involving trains, subways, or buses. Along with designing these types of systems, some transportation engineers might be involved in overseeing the actual construction of a project.

College training is a must for both traffic planners and transportation engineers. Degrees in civil engineering or urban planning are good choices for both of these professions. Many traffic planners find that a graduate degree with a specialization in areas such as traffic flow theory or freeway exit design helps prepare them for the challenges of the job. Almost half of all transportation engineers have earned graduate degrees,

and their studies might include topics such as engineering dynamics, surveying, and traffic control.

Once you start thinking about transportation-related careers, you can come up with a pretty long list of options. Add planes, ships, and other modes of transportation to the list and watch it really grow. Air traffic controllers, railroad engineers, logistics managers, pilots, ship captains, dispatchers, safety officers, mechanics, designers, and manufacturers are just a few of the careers that keep people and things moving.

You're bound to find a clear connection between math and many of these transportation-related careers. The problem solving, the logic, and the sheer numbers are all there in many different forms. So cracking those math books is a good way to prepare for an exciting career in transportation.

TRY IT OUT

MORE THAN ONE WAY AROUND THE BLOCK
How many ways can you get from your house to school? Go a different way every day for a week and keep track of how long it takes, how much traffic you encounter, how many stop lights you pass by, and other convenience and safety considerations. At the end of the week, rank the routes and recommend your favorites to friends who live nearby and to your favorite car pool drivers.

PLANES, TRAINS, AND AUTOMOBILES
Pick a mode of transportation and turn yourself into an expert by using some of the same skills that any seasoned traffic planner would use: observation and research. Choose from airplanes, boats, cars, trucks, trains, construction vehicles, motorcycles—anything that interests you. Then get a notebook and start collecting photographs, interesting facts and trivia, and your own ideas about how to make the most of your preferred method of transportation in our changing world.

ROADSIDE READING

Transport yourself to a far-reaching world of traffic- and transportation-related careers by browsing through some of the following books.

Heitzman, William Ray. *Opportunities in Marine and Maritime Careers.* Lincolnwood, Ill.: VGM Career Horizons, 1994.

March, Carol. *Choosing an Airline Career: In-Depth Descriptions of Entry-Level Positions, Travel Benefits, How to Apply and Interview.* New York: Capri Publishing, 1993.

Paradis, Adrian A. *Opportunities in Transportation Careers.* Lincolnwood, Ill.: VGM Career Horizons, 1997.

Rubin, Karen. *Flying High in Travel: A Complete Guide to Careers in the Travel Industry.* New York: John Wiley and Sons, 1992.

Schultz, Marjorie R. *Transportation.* New York: Franklin Watts, 1990.

On the more technical side are books specific to traffic engineering. You may not be ready to dive in and read these books from cover to cover yet, but they can give you a better idea of what traffic planners and engineers do.

Garber, Nicholas, and Lester A. Hoel. *Traffic and Highway Engineering.* Boston: PWS, 1997.

McShane, William R., et al. *Traffic Engineering.* Englewood Cliffs, N.J.: Prentice-Hall, 1997.

ON THE GO WITH UNCLE SAM

When it comes to careers in transportation, no one does it quite like the military. Nearly every mode of transportation is represented in one branch of service or another. The military uses sleek fighter jets and robot-powered tanks, not to mention ships and submarines. If it floats, flies, or moves on wheels, you're bound to find it in one of the branches of the armed forces.

To find out how to blend an interest in transportation with military service, check out some of these websites.

- ☼ U.S. Air Force at http://www.airforce.com
- ☼ U.S. Army at http://www.army.mil
- ☼ U.S. Coast Guard at http://www.uscg.mil/welcome.html
- ☼ U.S. Navy at http://www.navy.com
- ☼ U.S. Marines at http://www.marines.com

VIRTUAL CRUISING

The information highway is the place to look for serious information about traffic and transportation, as well as some transportation-related fun and games. Feel free to goof off at some of the sites listed below.

- ☼ Eavesdrop on live conversations between air traffic controllers and airline pilots at http://www.audionet.com/simuflite.
- ☼ Take a virtual subway trip on New York City's A line at http://www.multimedia.bell-labs.com/metaphorium/SS/aboutSS.html.
- ☼ Find links to transportation information geared toward young people of all ages at http://transweb.sjsu.edu/kidlinks.htm. Here you'll find links to sites such as the railroad games home page, the New York City Transit Museum, and TRACNet, a hands-on transportation engineering program designed for middle school and high school students.

When it's time to buckle down and get to business, try some of these sites to find out more about what traffic planners and transportation engineers do for a living.

- ☼ The National Transportation Library contains all kinds of documents and databases provided by transportation professionals. You can find this website at http://www.bts.gov/smart.

☯ The PATH (Partners for Advanced Transit and Highways) Database has all the latest research in intelligent transportation systems at http://www.nas.edu/trb/about/path1.html.

☯ The Transportation Internet Resource Directory provides links to all kinds of interesting websites at http://www.lib.berkeley.edu/ITSL/transres.html.

CHECK IT OUT

Aerospace and Transportation Education Association
P.O. Box 242273
Montgomery, Alabama 36124-2273
http://www.astea.org

American Society of Civil Engineers
1801 Alexander Bell Drive
Reston, Virginia 20191-4400
http://www.asce.org

Institute of Transportation Engineers
525 School Street SW, Suite 410
Washington, D.C. 20024
http://www.ite.org

Intelligent Transportation Society of America
400 Virginia Avenue SW, Suite 800
Washington, D.C. 20024
http://www.itsa.org

Transportation Research Board
National Academy of Sciences
2101 Constitution Avenue NW
Washington, D.C. 20418
http://www.nas.edu/trb/

GET ACQUAINTED

Jennifer Sherman,
Traffic Planner

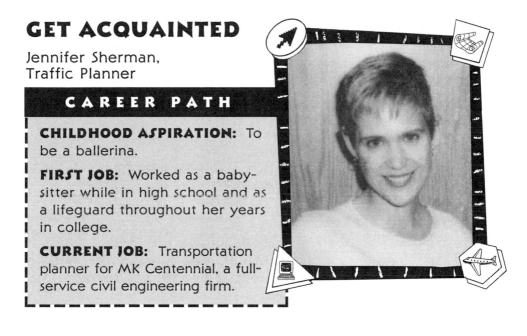

CAREER PATH

CHILDHOOD ASPIRATION: To be a ballerina.

FIRST JOB: Worked as a baby-sitter while in high school and as a lifeguard throughout her years in college.

CURRENT JOB: Transportation planner for MK Centennial, a full-service civil engineering firm.

AIRBORNE INSPIRATION

Jennifer Sherman says it was a series of strange coincidences that landed her in a career in transportation. While taking a high school economics class, Sherman was intrigued by a book called *Free to Choose* by Milton Friedman. You can imagine her surprise when she found herself sitting next to the author of that very book during an airline flight. Their subsequent in-flight conversation inspired her to pursue an economics degree when she went to college.

Sherman was sailing along in this program when in her senior year another strange incident occurred. She went to register for the upper-level economics class she needed to take to graduate and discovered it was already full. Desperate to solve this problem, she found out that an introductory course to transportation would give her the credit she needed, so she signed up without any idea of what to expect. As it turns out, Sherman loved the class and was so impressed with its professor that the next semester she took an urban transportation class he taught. By the time the class was over, she was seriously hooked.

Sherman's professor recognized her interest and exceptional abilities in this area (she was the best student in the class) and encouraged her to get a master's degree in urban regional planning with an emphasis in transportation. She followed his advice.

During the next two years, she learned more than she ever thought possible about traffic. She says math particularly came into play in several statistics classes that she took. Learning how to make population forecasts and traffic volume forecasts were key to doing the work she does now.

UP, UP, AND AWAY

After graduating, Sherman looked for a job in the aviation field and landed a position as an aviation planner with a regional council of governments. Her job was to generate reports for the airlines about airplane takeoffs and landings and other aspects of air traffic around the region. The job was all right, but it didn't keep her busy enough. She was getting bored with the job, when the manager of the traffic operations asked to "borrow" some of her time.

Working in the traffic operations department, she was assigned a project to determine the best traffic signal timing for various areas in the region. Her job was to find answers to questions such as

- How much traffic travels on specific roads at specific times of the day?
- How many seconds of green light time is needed to keep cars moving through each intersection efficiently?
- Which side of an intersection needs the most green time?
- How can lights along a corridor (route) be timed so that cars don't get stuck at every red light?

Sherman found that she really enjoyed the meticulous research and careful investigation required to answer those kinds of questions. It wasn't long before she had changed jobs and began focusing exclusively on ground transportation.

STEP BY STEP

Researching data about traffic patterns is just the first step in the traffic planning process. Once Sherman has the information she needs, she uses it to generate reports complete with her recommendations for solving various problems efficiently. Those statistics classes she took come in handy when her recommendations are based on such issues as travel time savings, fuel savings, air pollution reduction, and reduced number of total stops for drivers following a given route. Fortunately, there are some very sophisticated computer programs that help traffic planners figure it all out.

One particularly interesting project Sherman has worked on involved developing a traffic management plan for the major intersections near a sports arena in Denver. On game days thousands of fans typically jam the area and create a traffic scenario much different from an ordinary day. In order to implement a plan that could adapt to these wildly varying traffic patterns, the city decided to install an "intelligent" traffic management system using computer-operated signs that monitor traffic flow and relay the information to the city's traffic management center. Traffic managers at the center use computers to relay messages to the signs and change the traffic patterns accordingly. It's a high-tech solution to the old-fashioned traffic jam.

WHAT DO YOU DO FOR A LIVING?

When Sherman tells people about her job, the most common response is "I didn't know that anyone actually did that." Traffic lights are something that most people take for granted without considering the amount of work and expense that they generate. For instance, Sherman estimates that it can cost as much as $100,000 just to install traffic lights at one intersection. That doesn't include the extensive planning process or the expense of maintaining the lights. Remember that someone has to replace the bulbs when they burn out and repair the structures when they are damaged.

Urban Planner

WHAT IS AN URBAN PLANNER?

An urban planner works with one goal in mind: to make life better for people. An urban planner does this by creating environments that are functional, comfortable, convenient, healthy, efficient, and attractive. He or she must promote the best use of a community's land and resources for places for people to live, work, and play. Whether designing a beautiful park, curbing traffic congestion, or combating pollution, the urban planner applies creative solutions to complex problems that affect people and the world around them.

Urban planners work to make improvements that will meet the needs of people and their communities now and in the years to come. Their work may involve a single building, a neighborhood, a small town, a city, a county, or a metropolitan region. Sometimes they may be designing an entire city or neighborhood from scratch. Other times their work involves preserving historical landmarks or redeveloping decaying areas such as those in the older sections of a large city.

Regardless of the type of project, the single most important skill for urban planners is the ability to see the big picture. They must be able to capture a vision of all that a given project might involve and how it connects to all other aspects of a community. The next most important skill for planners is the ability to convey that vision to others in pictures and in words. To complete the picture part, most planners find that a blend of artistic creativity and computer savvy come in handy in illustrating and defining their project in a way that allows others to understand their ideas. Sharing their ideas in words requires excellent writing and speaking skills. Because the nature of their work often represents change and people tend to resist change, planners must present their ideas using diplomatic and persuasive communication skills.

Planners are often employed by government agencies of all sizes on a city, county, state, or federal level. They are also employed by architectural firms, engineering firms, and real-estate development companies. Depending on the nature of their responsibilities, planners may specialize in areas such as environmental planning, land-use planning, and water resource management. Their work often requires them to interface with architects, engineers, construction contractors, and other professionals who turn a planner's ideas into reality.

A college degree in urban planning, civil engineering, architecture, or public administration is required to get a job as an urban planner. Some planners find that a master's degree in a field such as structural engineering may become necessary if they wish to advance farther in their career.

Those who are interested in this type of work but prefer less training might consider related jobs such as surveyor, drafter, computer-aided design (CAD) specialist, or landscaper. The common thread that links these professions with urban planning is a desire to use creative skills to make the world a better and more beautiful place.

TRY IT OUT

KID TOWN, U.S.A.

Here's your chance to have things your way. Close your eyes and imagine a place where everything is geared for people just your age. The activities, the buildings, the stores, the modes of transportation—everything. Let your imagination go wild and focus on the details. Now, grab a notebook and pen, and make a list of all the special features of your wannabe, wish-it-could-be town. Use your ideas to create a poster or sketch so that others can share your vision for a town that's just right for kids like you.

Go a step further and build a model of your town using boxes. For complete instructions and lots of stretch-the-imagination planning activities, use Ginny and Dean Graves' fun resource entitled *Box City: An Interdisciplinary Experience in Community Planning* (Prairie Village, Kan.: Center for Understanding the Built Environment, 1999).

BUILD IT AND THEY WILL COME

If virtual reality is more your thing, you can create and run your own amazing city on the scale of San Francisco or Berlin with Sim City 3000, a computer software game published by Electronic Arts. You can find this game at most major toy or software stores or order it on-line at http://www.simcity.com/home.shtml.

READING BETWEEN THE BUILDINGS

The Center for Understanding the Built Environment (CUBE) is an organization that encourages young people to work together to create a quality-built and natural environment. Visit CUBE's website at http://www.cubekc.org where you'll find ideas for many activities including Reading a Building. This activity gives you a new look at familiar buildings, encouraging you to really notice details such as the walls, the roof, the windows, and the doors as well as special features such as arches, columns, and other ornaments.

You can use the chart found at http://www.cubekc.org/architivities/rab.htm to record your discoveries. As you observe the structure, remember that each of those features is a result of planning and design. See if you can get inside the designer's head and make some conclusions about why certain choices were made. How do all those elements come together to create a building that is well used and well loved?

MY TOWN IS BEST

For the sake of this activity, let's assume that you really like the place where you live. Suppose your job was to design a postcard enticing other people your age to come to visit your town. Start by spelling out the name of your town in big, fancy letters. Use each of the letters to illustrate or describe something that makes your town special. Feel free to use a computer program to help with the graphics. Just do everything you can to make it inviting and eye-catching.

For additional information and ideas, visit another one of CUBE's activity pages at http://www.cubekc.org/architivities/postcard.htm.

A STROLL AROUND TOWN

Take the time to walk through your town or neighborhood. Make the experience especially informative by bringing along a copy of *Walk Around the Block* by Ginny and Dean Graves and others (Prairie Village, Kans.: Center for Understanding the Built Environment, 1999). This workbook will guide you through an investigation of architectural design, city planning, preservation, history, economics, politics, geography, science, and art in your neck of the woods. You may be surprised by what you find.

URBAN PLANNING 101
The following books will start you on your quest for knowledge about urban planning.

Glenn, Patricia Brown. *Discover America's Favorite Architects.* New York: John Wiley and Sons, 1996.
———. *Under One Roof.* Washington, D.C.: Preservation Press, 1993.

Some websites worth a visit include

☀ Virtual Museum of Architecture at http://www.quon-dam.com
☀ The National Trust's National Main Street Center at http://www.mainst.org

WELCOME TO WALTOPIA
If anyone ever had grand plans for great cities, it was Walt Disney. Creator of Mickey Mouse and founder of the Disneyland and Walt Disney World entertainment empire, this man dared to dream big dreams and, even better, had the courage to make them happen. Epcot, another part of the Disney entertainment empire, began as Walt Disney's dream of a perfect city. You can get a look at Disney's original plans, as well as photographs of the result of that dream, at an award-winning website called Waltopia. Find it at http://home.earthlink.net/~p_williams/body.html.

CHECK IT OUT

Alliance for National Renewal
National Civic League
1445 Market Street, Suite 300
Denver, Colorado 80202-1728

American Institute of Architects
1735 New York Avenue NW
Washington, D.C. 20006
http://www.e-architect.com

American Institute of Certified Planners
1776 Massachusetts Avenue NW
Washington, D.C. 20077-5824
http://www.planning.org

American Planning Association
122 South Michigan Avenue, Suite 1600
Chicago, Illinois 60603
http://www.planning.org

Center for Understanding the Built Environment (CUBE)
5328 West 67th Street
Prairie Village, Kansas 66208
http://www.webcom.com/~pcj/cube.html

Planning and Design Institute
231 East Buffalo Street, Suite 100
Milwaukee, Wisconsin 53202
http://www.pdisite.com

Student Planning Association
Department of City Planning
College of Architecture
Georgia Institute of Technology
Atlanta, Georgia 30332-0155
http://www.arch.gatech.edu/~spa

Urban Land Institute
1025 Thomas Jefferson Street NW, Suite 500W
Washington, D.C. 20007

GET ACQUAINTED

Ramona Mullahey,
Urban Planner

CAREER PATH

CHILDHOOD ASPIRATION: To be a mathematician.

FIRST JOB: Junior science apprentice at the University of Hawaii during her junior year of high school.

CURRENT JOB: Community builder fellow for the Urban Peace Corps, a federally funded program of the Department of Housing and Urban Development.

IT DIDN'T ADD UP

Ramona Mullahey was named after her aunt, a math teacher. Wanting to live up to the honor of her name, Mullahey took all the math classes she could in high school and went to college with the intention of following in her aunt's footsteps as a mathematician. On the way to getting her degree, she discovered something important. Math wasn't the right choice for her. Sure, she liked math and she was good at it, but there was another side to her that didn't want there to be just one right answer all the time.

She ended up switching to a political science major, which is often used as a stepping stone for law school. But in order to get into law school, you have to pass a really tough exam. Mullahey took the exam and flunked it—twice. So much for that idea.

Although the experience was unpleasant, it reinforced the idea that Mullahey just wasn't cut out for work that required her to fit all the answers into a neat little box. She worked best

146

when she could be creative and find different ways to solve problems and use information.

THIS IS IT!
Mullahey found the perfect fit when she was thumbing through a college catalog. The college offered programs in planning and architecture. Working with people to shape communities was one of the ways the catalog described the careers associated with the degrees. That concept clicked with Mullahey in a big way. She says it completely resonated with who she was and what she wanted to do with her life. She decided to go for it and has never looked back.

ALOHA COMMUNITIES
Mullahey was born and raised in Hawaii. She says that one of the most satisfying parts of her work as a planner has involved historic and cultural preservation projects. While the work is important for honoring the traditions of the past, it also helps give people a sense of who they are and a respect for where they are. For this reason, one project in particular was especially rewarding for Mullahey.

This project involved cleaning and restoring the site of a heiau, a native Hawaiian religious place. Originally the site had been considered sacred and was marked by monuments made of stone. When Mullahey and her team came on the scene, the site was overwhelmed by trash and overgrown with weeds. It was no small task returning the site back to a place of distinction. Mullahey relied on a group of hardworking partners from government, business, the nonprofit sector, and the community to do the dirty work. Their efforts paid off when the project was honored with an award from the National Trust for Historic Preservation.

CREATING A NEW TOWN
Another big project that Mullahey has worked on involved transforming what had long been a rural sugarcane town on the island of Oahu into a thriving suburban city. The project

has an eventual goal of providing affordable and market housing for 120,000 people. It involves building neighborhoods, schools, businesses, shopping malls, and all the other places that mark a small city.

Mullahey's involvement in this project included three phases. Her first task was to educate the existing community about what planning is all about and what the new project would mean for them. She did this by working with teachers and schools to help students create a Box City (see the Try It Out activity mentioned earlier) version of the new community. This phase also involved working with city council, landowners, and citizens who had concerns about the impact of the development on their businesses and neighborhoods.

The second phase involved what Mullahey calls community building activities. The new city, named Kapolei, was just that— new. Mullahey's job was to help establish traditions that would pull people together. One way that Mullahey did this was by organizing seasonal celebrations and festivals that brought people together with food and fun. Over time, these types of activities can create a thread of tradition that helps bind people together in a common experience. And that's what community is all about.

The third way that Mullahey has been involved in the Kapolei project was in the community's new elementary school. She helped organize volunteers and round up business support in ways that brought them together to create a stronger and better school for their community.

For Mullahey, planning communities is less about building structures and more about creating good places for people to live.

MAKE A DETOUR THAT COUNTS!

Math leads the way to countless career opportunities. Math's natural affinity to technology and science leads to an interesting array of options. Go through these lists of suggested careers and see if some sound right for you. If you're not familiar with one of them, or if one (or more!) sounds particularly intriguing, look it up in one of the career encyclopedias listed on page 178.

A WORLD OF MATHEMATICAL CAREERS

IT'S A HIGH-TECH WORLD
Remember that math drives the high-tech world in which we live. These careers blend math with computer skills.

artificial intelligence specialist
computer analyst
computer-assisted design
  (CAD) specialist
computer engineer

computer scientist
cryptanalyst
operations manager
operations research analyst
telecommunications technician

THE DYNAMIC DUO: MATH AND SCIENCE
The following careers combine math with science.

agronomist
astronomer
astrophysicist
biologist
biomedical engineer
chemist
climatologist

conservationist
ecologist
geodesist
geologist
hydrologist
meteorologist
physicist

ENGINEERING AN EXCITING CAREER
Engineers are at the forefront of all kinds of discovery, and engineering careers are based on many interests, including math.

aerospace engineer
agricultural engineer
automotive engineer
biomedical engineer
ceramic engineer
computer engineer
environmental engineer
industrial engineer

mechanical engineer
metallurgy engineer
mining engineer
naval engineer
nuclear engineer
petroleum engineer
robotics engineer

SOME HEALTH-MINDED CHOICES

A solid math background is essential for success in all these medical professions.

chiropractor
clinical lab technician
dental hygienist
dentist
health administrator
nurse

optician
optometrist
physical therapist
physician
respiratory therapist
surgeon

IN THE NUMBERS BUSINESS

Making sure the numbers add up in the business world is at the heart of these careers.

accountant
auditor
demographer
estimator
financial analyst
insurance underwriter

labor negotiator
market analyst
printer
real estate appraiser
zoning inspector

ON THE MOVE

Math is important for careers related to all modes of transportation.

aerial photographer
aeronautical engineer
airline cargo manager
air traffic controller
avionics technician
logistics manager
merchant marine captain
merchant marine purser
railroad engineer
railroad signaler
truck and bus dispatcher

INFORMATION IS POWER

Mind-boggling, isn't it? There are so many great choices, so many jobs you've never heard of before. How will you ever narrow it down to the perfect spot for you?

First, pinpoint the ideas that sound the most interesting to you. Then, find out all you can about them. As you may have noticed, a similar pattern of information was used for each of the career entries featured in this book. Each entry included

☞ a general description or definition of the career
☞ some hands-on projects that give readers a chance to actually experience a job
☞ a list of organizations to contact for more information
☞ an interview with a professional

You can use information like this to help you determine the best career path to pursue. Since there isn't room in one book to profile all these math-related career choices, here's your chance to do it yourself. Conduct a full investigation into a math career that interests you.

Please Note: If this book does not belong to you, use a separate sheet of paper to record your responses to the following questions.

CAREER TITLE_____

WHAT IS A _____?

Use career encyclopedias and other resources to write a description of this career.

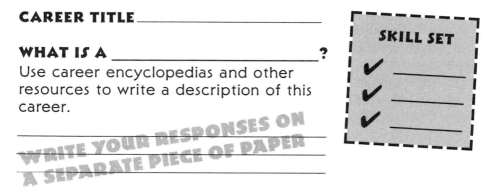

SKILL SET

✔ _____
✔ _____
✔ _____

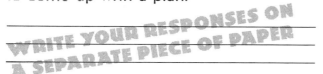

TRY IT OUT

Write project ideas here. Ask your parents and your teacher to come up with a plan.

CHECK IT OUT

List professional organizations where you can learn more about this profession.

GET ACQUAINTED

Interview a professional in the field and summarize your findings.

WRITE YOUR RESPONSES ON A SEPARATE PIECE OF PAPER

DON'T STOP NOW!
GO FOR IT!

It's been a fast-paced trip so far. Take a break, regroup, and look at all the progress you've made.

1st Stop: Self-Discovery
You discovered some personal interests and natural abilities that you can start building a career around.

2nd Stop: Exploration
You've explored an exciting array of career opportunities in math. You're now aware that your career can involve either a specialized area with many educational requirements or that it can involve a practical application of skills with a minimum of training and experience.

At this point, you've found a couple of (or few) careers that really intrigue you. Now it's time to put it all together and do all you can to make an informed, intelligent choice. It's time to move on.

3rd Stop: Experimentation

By the time you finish this section, you'll have reached one of three points in the career planning process.

1. **Green light!** You found it. No need to look any further. This is *the* career for you. (This may happen to a lucky few. Don't worry if it hasn't happened yet for you. This whole process is about exploring options, experimenting with ideas, and, eventually, making the best choice for you.)

2. **Yellow light!** Close, but not quite. You seem to be on the right path but you haven't nailed things down for sure. (This is where many people your age end up, and it's a good place to be. You've learned what it takes to really check things out. Hang in there. Your time will come.)

3. **Red light!** Whoa! No doubt about it, this career just isn't for you. (Congratulations! Aren't you glad you found out now and not after you'd spent four years in college preparing for this career? Your next stop: Make a U-turn and start this process over with another career.)

Here's a sneak peek at what you'll be doing in the next section.

❀ First, you'll pick a favorite career idea (or two or three).

❀ Second, you'll snoop around the library to find answers to the 10 things you've just got to know about your future career.

❀ Third, you'll pick up the phone and talk to someone whose career you admire to find out what it's really like.

❀ Fourth, you'll link up with a whole world of great information about your career idea on the Internet (it's easier than you think).

❀ Fifth, you'll go on the job to shadow a professional for a day.

Hang on to your hats and get ready to make tracks!

#1 NARROW DOWN YOUR CHOICES

You've been introduced to quite a few math career ideas. You may also have some ideas of your own to add. Which ones appeal to you the most?

Write your top three choices in the spaces below. (Sorry if this is starting to sound like a broken record, but . . . **if this book does not belong to you, write your responses on a separate sheet of paper.**)

1. _____
2. _____
3. _____

WRITE YOUR RESPONSES ON A SEPARATE PIECE OF PAPER

#2 SNOOP AT THE LIBRARY

Take your list of favorite career ideas, a notebook, and a helpful adult with you to the library. When you get there, go to the reference section and ask the librarian to help you find

books about careers. Most libraries will have at least one set of career encyclopedias. Some of the larger libraries may also have career information on CD-ROM.

Gather all the information you can and use it to answer the following questions in your notebook about each of the careers on your list. Make sure to ask for help if you get stuck.

TOP 10 THINGS YOU NEED TO KNOW ABOUT YOUR CAREER

1. What kinds of skills does this job require?
2. What kind of training is required? (Compare the options for a high school degree, trade school degree, two-year degree, four-year degree, and advanced degree.)
3. What types of classes do I need to take in high school in order to be accepted into a training program?
4. What are the names of three schools or colleges where I can get the training I need?
5. Are there any apprenticeship or internship opportunities available? If so, where? If not, could I create my own opportunity? How?
6. How much money can I expect to earn as a beginner? How much with more experience?
7. What kinds of places hire people to do this kind of work?
8. What is a typical work environment like? For example, would I work in a busy office, outdoors, or in a laboratory?
9. What are some books and magazines I could read to learn more about this career? Make a list and look for them at your library.
10. Where can I write for more information? Make a list of professional associations.

#3 CHAT ON THE PHONE

Talking to a seasoned professional—someone who experiences the job day in and day out—can be a great way to get the inside story on what a career is all about. Fortunately for you, the experts in any career field can be as close as the nearest telephone.

Sure it can be a bit scary calling up an adult whom you don't know. But, two things are in your favor:

1. They can't see you. The worst thing they can do is hang up on you, so just relax and enjoy the conversation.
2. They'll probably be happy to talk to you about their job. In fact, most people will be flattered that you've called. If you happen to contact someone who seems reluctant to talk, thank them for their time and try someone else.

Here are a few pointers to help make your telephone interview a success.

- ☼ Mind your manners and speak clearly.
- ☼ Be respectful of their time and position.
- ☼ Be prepared with good questions and take notes as you talk.

One more commonsense reminder: Be careful about giving out your address and DO NOT arrange to meet anyone you don't know without your parents' supervision.

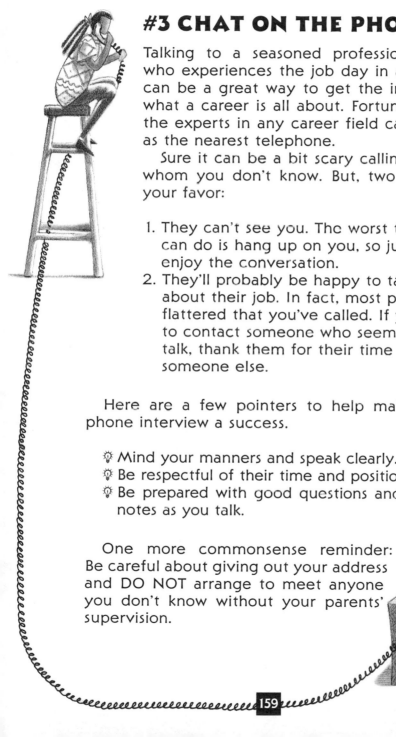

TRACKING DOWN CAREER EXPERTS

You might be wondering by now how to find someone to interview. Have no fear! It's easy, if you're persistent. All you have to do is ask. Ask the right people and you'll have a great lead in no time.

A few of the people to ask and sources to turn to are

Your parents. They may know someone (or know someone who knows someone) who has just the kind of job you're looking for.

Your friends and neighbors. You might be surprised to find out how many interesting jobs these people have when you start asking them what they (or their parents) do for a living.

Librarians. Since you've already figured out what kinds of companies employ people in your field of interest, the next step is to ask for information about local employers. Although it's a bit cumbersome to use, a big volume called *Contacts Influential* can provide this kind of information.

Professional associations. Call or write to the professional associations you discovered in Activity #1 a few pages back and ask for recommendations.

Chambers of commerce. The local chamber of commerce probably has a directory of employers, their specialties, and their phone numbers. Call the chamber, explain what you are looking for, and give the person a chance to help the future workforce.

Newspaper and magazine articles. Find an article about the subject you are interested in. Chances are pretty good that it will mention the name of at least one expert in the field. The article probably won't include the person's phone number (that would be too easy), so you'll have to look for clues. Common clues include the name of the company that the expert works for, the town that he or she lives in, and if the person is an author, the name of his or her publisher. Make a few phone calls and track the person down (if long distance calls are involved, make sure to get your parents' permission first).

INQUIRING KIDS WANT TO KNOW

Before you make the call, make a list of questions to ask. You'll cover more ground if you focus on using the five w's (and the h) that you've probably heard about in your creative writing classes: Who? What? Where? When? How? and Why? For example,

1. Who do you work for?
2. What is a typical work day like for you?
3. Where can I get some on-the-job experience?
4. When did you become a _____?
   (profession)
5. How much can you earn in this profession? (But, remember it's not polite to ask someone how much *he* or *she* earns.)
6. Why did you choose this profession?

One last suggestion: Add a professional (and very classy) touch to the interview process by following up with a thank-you note to the person who took time out of a busy schedule to talk with you.

#4 SURF THE NET

With the Internet, the new information super-highway, charging full steam ahead, you literally have a world of information at your fingertips. The Internet has something for everyone, and it's getting easier to access all the time. An increasing number of libraries and schools are offering access to the Internet on their computers. In addition, companies such as America Online and CompuServe have made it possible for anyone with a home computer to surf the World Wide Web.

A typical career search will land everything from the latest news on developments in the field and course notes from universities to museum exhibits, interactive games, educational activities, and more. You just can't beat the timeliness or the variety of information available on the Net.

One of the easiest ways to track down this information is to use an Internet search engine, such as Yahoo! Simply type in the topic you are looking for, and in a matter of seconds, you'll have a list of options from around the world. It's fun to browse—you never know what you'll come up with.

To narrow down your search a bit, look for specific websites, forums, or chatrooms that are related to your topic in the following publications:

Gentry, Lorna, Mark Bibler, and Kelli Brooks. *New Rider's Official Internet and World Wide Web Yellow Pages.* Indianapolis, Ind.: New Rider's Publishing, 1998.

Hahn, Harley. *Harley Hahn's Internet and Web Yellow Pages.* Berkeley, Calif.: Osborne McGraw Hill, 1998.

Maxwell, Christine. *Internet Yellow Pages.* Indianapolis, Ind.: New Rider's Publishing, 1997.

Polly, Jean Armour. *The Internet Kids and Family Yellow Pages.* Berkeley, Calif.: Osborne McGraw Hill, 1998.

To go on-line at home you may want to compare two of the more popular on-line services: America Online and CompuServe. Please note that there is a monthly subscription fee for using these services. There can also be extra fees attached to specific forums and services, so *make sure you have your parents' OK before you sign up.* For information about America Online call 800-827-6364. For information

about CompuServe call 800-848-8990. Both services frequently offer free start-up deals, so shop around.

There are also many other services, depending on where you live. Check your local phone book or ads in local computer magazines for other service options.

Before you link up, keep in mind that many of these sites are geared toward professionals who are already working in a particular field. Some of the sites can get pretty technical. Just use the experience as a chance to nose around the field, hang out with the people who are tops in the field, and think about whether or not you'd like to be involved in a profession like that.

Specific sites to look for are the following:

Professional associations. Find out about what's happening in the field, conferences, journals, and other helpful tidbits.

Schools that specialize in this area. Many include research tools, introductory courses, and all kinds of interesting information.

Government agencies. Quite a few are going high-tech with lots of helpful resources.

Websites hosted by experts in the field (this seems to be a popular hobby among many professionals). These websites are often as entertaining as they are informative.

If you're not sure where to go, just start clicking around. Sites often link to other sites. You may want to jot down notes about favorite sites. Sometimes you can even print out information that isn't copyright-protected; try the print option and see what happens.

Be prepared: Surfing the Internet can be an addicting habit! There is so much great information. It's a fun way to focus on your future.

#5 SHADOW A PROFESSIONAL

Linking up with someone who is gainfully employed in a profession that you want to explore is a great way to find out what a career is like. Following someone around while the person are at work is called "shadowing." Try it!

This process involves three steps.

1. Find someone to shadow. Some suggestions include

   ☼ the person you interviewed (if you enjoyed talking with him or her and feel comfortable about asking the person to show you around the workplace)

   ☼ friends and neighbors (you may even be shocked to discover that your parents have interesting jobs)

   ☼ workers at the chamber of commerce may know of mentoring programs available in your area (it's a popular concept, so most larger areas should have something going on)

   ☼ someone at your local School-to-Work office, the local Boy Scouts Explorer program director (this is available to girls too!), or your school guidance counselor

2. Make a date. Call and make an appointment. Find out when is the best time for arrival and departure. Make arrangements with a parent or other respected adult to go with you and get there on time.

3. Keep your ears and eyes open. This is one time when it is OK to be nosy. Ask

questions. Notice everything that is happening around you. Ask your host to let you try some of the tasks he or she is doing.

The basic idea of the shadowing experience is to put yourself in the other person's shoes and see how they fit. Imagine yourself having a job like this 10 or 15 years down the road. It's a great way to find out if you are suited for a particular line of work.

BE CAREFUL OUT THERE!

Two cautions must accompany this recommendation. First, remember the stranger danger rules of your childhood. NEVER meet with anyone you don't know without your parents' permission and ALWAYS meet in a supervised situation—at the office or with your parents.

Second, be careful not to overdo it. These people are busy earning a living, so respect their time by limiting your contact and coming prepared with valid questions and background information.

PLAN B

If shadowing opportunities are limited where you live, try one of these approaches for learning the ropes from a professional.

Pen pals. Find a mentor who is willing to share information, send interesting materials, or answer specific questions that come up during your search.

Cyber pals. Go on-line in a forum or chatroom related to your profession. You'll be able to chat with professionals from all over the world.

If you want to get some more on-the-job experience, try one of these approaches.

Volunteer to do the dirty work. Volunteer to work for someone who has a job that interests you for a specified period of time. Do anything—filing, errands, emptying trash cans—that puts you in contact with professionals. Notice every tiny detail about the profession. Listen to the lingo they use in the profession. Watch how they perform their jobs on a day-to-day basis.

Be an apprentice. This centuries-old job training method is making a comeback. Find out if you can set up an official on-the-job training program to gain valuable experience. Ask professional associations about apprenticeship opportunities. Once again, a School-to-Work program can be a great asset. In many areas, they've established some very interesting career training opportunities.

Hire yourself for the job. Maybe you are simply too young to do much in the way of on-the-job training right now. That's OK. Start learning all you can now and you'll be ready to really wow them when the time is right. Make sure you do all the Try It Out activities included for the career(s) you are most interested in. Use those activities as a starting point for creating other projects that will give you a feel for what the job is like.

WHAT'S NEXT?

Have you carefully worked your way through all of the suggested activities? You haven't tried to sneak past anything, have you? This isn't a place for shortcuts. If you've done the activities, you're ready to decide where you stand with each career idea. So what is it? Green light? See page 170. Yellow light? See page 169. Red light? See page 168. Find the spot that best describes your response to what you've discovered about this career idea and plan your next move.

RED LIGHT

So you've decided this career is definitely not for you—hang in there! The process of elimination is an important one. You've learned some valuable career planning skills; use them to explore other ideas. In the meantime, use the following road map to chart a plan to get beyond this "spinning your wheels" point in the process.

Take a variety of classes at school to expose yourself to new ideas and expand the options. Make a list of courses you want to try.

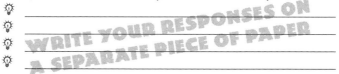

Get involved in clubs and other after-school activities (like 4-H or Boy Scout Explorers) to further develop your interests. Write down some that interest you.

Read all you can find about interesting people and their work. Make a list of people you'd like to learn more about.

Keep at it. Time is on your side. Finding the perfect work for you is worth a little effort. Once you've crossed this hurdle, move on to the next pages and continue mapping out a great future.

YELLOW LIGHT

Proceed with caution. While the idea continues to intrigue you, you may wonder if it's the best choice for you. Your concerns are legitimate (listen to that nagging little voice inside!).

Maybe it's the training requirements that intimidate you. Maybe you have concerns about finding a good job once you complete the training. Maybe you wonder if you have what it takes to do the job.

At this point, it's good to remember that there is often more than one way to get somewhere. Check out all the choices and choose the route that's best for you. Use the following road map to move on down the road in your career planning adventure.

Make two lists. On the first, list the things you like most about the career you are currently investigating. On the second, list the things that are most important to you in a future career. Look for similarities on both lists and focus on careers that emphasize these similar key points.

Current Career	Future Career
☼ _____	☼ _____
☼ _____	☼ _____

What are some career ideas that are similar to the one you have in mind? Find out all you can about them. Go back through the exploration process explained on pages 157 to 166 and repeat some of the exercises that were most valuable.

☼ _____

☼ _____

☼ _____

☼ _____

Visit your school counselor and ask him or her which career assessment tools are available through your school. Use these to find out more about your strengths and interests. List the date, time, and place for any assessment tests you plan to take.

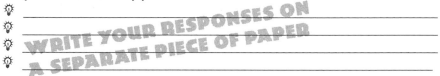

What other adults do you know and respect to whom you can talk about your future? They may have ideas that you've never thought of.

What kinds of part-time jobs, volunteer work, or after-school experiences can you look into that will give you a chance to build your skills and test your abilities? Think about how you can tap into these opportunities.

GREEN LIGHT

Yahoo! You are totally turned on to this career idea and ready to do whatever it takes to make it your life's work. Go for it!

Find out what kinds of classes you need to take now to prepare for this career. List them here.

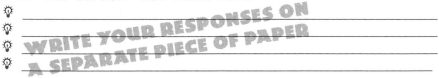

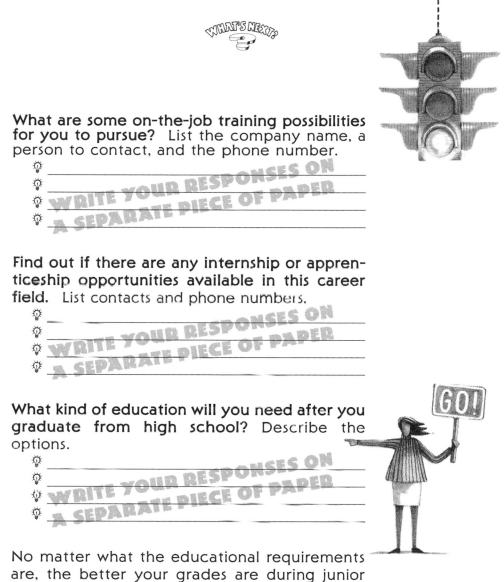

What are some on-the-job training possibilities for you to pursue? List the company name, a person to contact, and the phone number.

- _____
- _____
- _____
- _____

Find out if there are any internship or apprenticeship opportunities available in this career field. List contacts and phone numbers.

- _____
- _____
- _____
- _____

What kind of education will you need after you graduate from high school? Describe the options.

- _____
- _____
- _____
- _____

No matter what the educational requirements are, the better your grades are during junior and senior high school, the better your chances for the future.

Take a minute to think about some areas that need improvement in your schoolwork. Write your goals for giving it all you've got here.

- _____
- _____
- _____
- _____

Where can you get the training you'll need? Make a list of colleges, technical schools, or vocational programs. Include addresses so that you can write to request a catalog.

WRITE YOUR RESPONSES ON A SEPARATE PIECE OF PAPER

HOORAY! YOU DID IT!

This has been quite a trip. If someone tries to tell you that this process is easy, don't believe it. Figuring out what you want to do with the rest of your life is heavy stuff, and it should be. If you don't put some thought (and some sweat and hard work) into the process, you'll get stuck with whatever comes your way.

You may not have things planned to a T. Actually, it's probably better if you don't. You'll change some of your ideas as you grow and experience new things. And, you may find an interesting detour or two along the way. That's OK.

The most important thing about beginning this process now is that you've started to dream. You've discovered that you have some unique talents and abilities to share. You've become aware of some of the ways you can use them to make a living—and, perhaps, make a difference in the world.

Whatever you do, don't lose sight of the hopes and dreams you've discovered. You've got your entire future ahead of you. Use it wisely.

SOME FUTURE DESTINATIONS

Wow! You've really made tracks during this whole process. Now that you've gotten this far, you'll want to keep moving forward to a great future. This section will point you toward some useful resources to help you make a conscientious career choice (that's just the opposite of falling into any old job on a fluke).

IT'S NOT JUST FOR NERDS

The school counselor's office is not just a place where teachers send troublemakers. One of its main purposes is to help students like you make the most of your educational opportunities. Most schools will have a number of useful resources, including career assessment tools (ask about the Self-Directed Search Career Explorer or the COPS Interest Inventory—these are especially useful assessments for people your age). There may also be a stash of books, videos, and other helpful materials.

Make sure no one's looking and sneak into your school counseling office to get some expert advice!

AWESOME INTERNET CAREER RESOURCES

Your parents will be green with envy when they see all the career planning resources you have at your fingertips. Get ready to hear them whine, "But they didn't have all this stuff when I was a kid." Make the most of these cyberspace opportunities.

- ☼ The Career Center for Teens (a site sponsored by Public Television Outreach) includes activities and information on 21st-century career opportunities. Find it at http://www.pbs.org/jobs/teenindex.html.
- ☼ Future Scan includes in-depth profiles on a wide variety of career choices and expert advice from their "Guidance Gurus." Check it out at http://www.futurescan.com.
- ☼ Two sites—Kaplan (http://www.kaplan.com) and Princeton Review (http://www.review.com)—include information about specific careers as well as all kinds of information about the education you'll need to prepare for your career of choice.
- ☼ JobStar California Career Guides is another site to explore specific career choices. Look for it at http://www.job-smart.org/tools/career/spec-car.htm.

IT'S NOT JUST FOR BOYS

Boys and girls alike are encouraged to contact their local version of the Boy Scouts Explorer program. It offers exciting on-the-job training experiences in a variety of professional fields. Look in the white pages of your community phone book for the local Boy Scouts of America program.

MORE CAREER BOOKS ESPECIALLY FOR NUMBER CRUNCHERS

There are a surprising number of ways to earn a living using mathematical skills. The following books provide more information about additional math-related career options.

Burnett, Rebecca. *Careers for Number Crunchers.* Lincolnwood, Ill.: VGM Career Horizons, 1992.

Fischgrund, Tom. *The Insider's Guide to the Top 20 Careers in Business and Management: What It's Really Like to Work in Advertising, Computers, Banking, Management.* New York: McGraw-Hill, 1993.

Haddock, Patricia. *Careers in Banking and Finance.* New York: Rosen Publishing, 1997.

Huffman, Harry. *Math for Business Careers.* New York: Macmillan/McGraw-Hill, 1995.

Kantranowitz, Mark, and Joann P. Degennaro. *The Prentice Hall Guide to Scholarships and Fellowships for Mathematics and Science. A Resource for Students Pursuing Careers in Mathematical Science.* New York: Prentice Hall, 1993.

Kaplan, Andrew. *Careers for Number Lovers.* Brookfield, Conn.: Millbrook Press, 1991.

Lambert, Stephen E., and Ruth Decotis. *Great Jobs for Math Majors.* Lincolnwood, Ill.: NTC Publishing Group, 1998.

Naficy, Mariam. *The Fast Track: The Insider's Guide to Winning Jobs in Management Consulting, Investment Banking, and Securities Trading.* New York: Broadway Books, 1997.

Paradis, Adrian A. *Opportunities in Banking Careers.* Lincolnwood, Ill.: VGM Career Horizons, 1993.

Parker, Marla. *She Does Math!: Real Life Problems from Women on the Job.* Washington, D.C.: Mathematical Association of America, 1995.

Richardson, Peter. *Great Careers for People Intersted in Math and Computers.* Detroit: UXL, 1997.

Ring, Trudy. *Careers in Finance.* Lincolnwood, Ill.: VGM Career Horizons, 1993.

Seeking Employment in the Mathematical Sciences. Providence, R.I.: Mathematical Sciences Employment Register, 1994.

Sterrett, Andrew. *101 Careers in Mathematics.* Washington, D.C.: Mathematical Association of America, 1996.

HEAVY-DUTY RESOURCES

Career encyclopedias provide general information about a lot of professions and can be a great place to start a career search. Those listed here are easy to use and provide useful information about nearly a zillion different jobs. Look for them in the reference section of your local library.

Cosgrove, Holli, ed. *Career Discovery Encyclopedia: 1997 Edition.* Chicago: J. G. Ferguson Publishing Company, 1997.

Encyclopedia of Career Choices for the 1990's. New York: Perigee Books/Putnam Publishing Group, 1992.

Maze, Marilyn, and Donald Mayall. *The Enhanced Guide for Occupational Exploration: Descriptions for the 2,800 Most Important Jobs.* Indianapolis: JIST, 1995.

VGM's Careers Encyclopedia. Lincolnwood, Ill.: VGM Career Books, 1997.

FINDING PLACES TO WORK

Use resources like these to find leads on local businesses, mentors, job shadowing opportunities, and internships. Later, use these same resources to find a great job!

Job Bank Guide to Computer Companies. Holbrook, Mass.:
  Adams Media Group, 1997.
*Peterson's Job Opportunities in Engineering and Technology
  1997.* Princeton, N.J.: Peterson's Guides, 1996.
LeCompte, Michelle. *Job Hunter's Sourcebook: Where to Find
  Employment Leads and Other Job Search Resources.*
  Detroit: Gale Research, 1996.

Also consult the Job Bank series (Holbrook, Mass.: Adams
Media Group). Adams publishes separate guides for Atlanta,
Seattle, and many major points in between. Ask your local
librarian if the library has a guide for the biggest city near you.

FINDING PLACES TO PRACTICE
JOB SKILLS

An apprenticeship is an official opportunity to learn a specific profession by working side by side with a skilled professional. As a training method, it's as old as the hills, and it's
making a comeback in a big way because people are realiz-
ing that doing a job is simply the best way to learn a job.

An internship is an official opportunity to gain
work experience (paid or unpaid) in an industry of interest. Interns are more likely to
be given entry-level tasks but often
have the chance to rub elbows with
people in key positions within a
company. In comparison to an
apprenticeship, which offers very
detailed training for a specific job, an
internship offers a broader look at a
particular kind of work environment.

Both are great ways to learn the
ropes and stay one step ahead of the
competition. Consider it dress rehearsal
for the real thing!

Landes, Michael. *The Back Door Guide to Short Term Job Adventures: Internships, Extraordinary Experiences, Seasonal Jobs, Volunteering, Work Abroad.* Berkeley, Calif.: Ten Speed Press, 1997.

Oldman, Mark, and Samer Hamadeh. *America's Top Internships.* New York: Princeton Review, 1998.

——. *The Internship Bible.* New York: Princeton Review, 1998.

Peterson's Internships 1999: More Than 50,000 Opportunities to Get an Edge in Today's Competitive Job Market. Princeton, N.J.: Peterson's Guides, 1998.

Srinivasan, Kalpana. *The Yale Daily News Guide to Internships.* New York: Simon and Schuster, 1998.

NO-COLLEGE OCCUPATIONS

Some of you will be relieved to learn that a college degree is not the only route to a satisfying, well-paying career. Whew! If you'd rather skip some of the schooling and get down to work, here are some books you need to consult.

Abrams, Kathleen S. *Guide to Careers Without College.* Danbury, Conn.: Franklin Watts, 1995.

Corwen, Leonard. *Careers Without College.* New York: Simon and Schuster, 1995.

——. *College Not Required!: 100 Great Careers That Don't Require a College Degree.* New York: Macmillan, 1995.

Farr, J. Michael. *America's Top Jobs for People Without College Degrees.* Indianapolis: JIST, 1997.

Jakubiak, J. *Specialty Occupational Outlook: Trade and Technical.* Detroit: Gale Research, 1996.

Murphy, John. *Success Without a College Degree: The Secrets of How to Get Ahead and Show Them All.* Kent, Wash.: Achievement Dynamics, 1997.

Stoddard, Brooke C. *Careers Without College: Building.* Princeton, N.J.: Peterson's Guides, 1994.

Unger, Harlow G. *But What If I Don't Want to Go to College?: A Guide to Success through Alternative Education.* Rev. ed. New York: Facts On File, 1998.

INDEX

Page numbers in **boldface** indicate main articles. Page numbers in *italics* indicate photographs.